A CHILD FROM THE VILLAGE

Middle East Literature in Translation
Michael Beard *and* Adnan Haydar, Series Editors

A CHILD FROM THE VILLAGE

Sayyid Qutb

Edited, Translated, and with an Introduction by
John Calvert *and* William Shepard

SYRACUSE UNIVERSITY PRESS

Originally published in Arabic as *Tifl min-al-Qarya* (Cairo: Dar al-Shuruq, 1946).

∞ The paper used in this publication meets the minimum requirements
of the American National Standard for Information Sciences—Permanence
of Paper for Printed Library Materials, ANSI Z39.48-1992.

For a listing of books published and distributed by Syracuse University Press,
visit www.SyracuseUniversityPress.syr.edu.

ISBN: 978-0-8156-0805-9 (cloth)
978-0-8156-1075-5 (paperback)   978-0-8156-0807-3 (e-book)

Library of Congress has cataloged the cloth edition as follows:
Qutb, Sayyid, 1903–1966.
  [Tifl min al-qaryah. English]
  A child from the village / Sayyid Qutb ; translated, edited, and with an
introduction by John Calvert and William Shepard.— 1st ed.
      p. cm. — (Middle East literature in translation)
  Includes bibliographical references.
  ISBN 0-8156-0805-5 (hardcover (cloth) : alk. paper)
  1. Autobiographical fiction, Arabic—Translations into English. I. Calvert, John,
Dr. II. Shepard, William E., 1933– III. Title. IV. Series.
  PJ7858.U8T513 2004
  892′.736—dc22   2004018792

Manufactured in the United States of America

To the author of *The Days*,[1] Dr. Taha Hussein Bey.

These, dear sir, are "days" like your "days," lived by a village child;
some are similar to your days and some are different.
The difference reflects the difference between one generation and another,
one village and another, one life and another, indeed the difference between
one nature and another, between one attitude and another.
But they are, when all is said and done, also "days."

Sayyid Qutb was born in 1906 in Musha, Asyut Province, Upper Egypt, the village of the title. After an early career as a poet and literary and social critic, he became a committed Islamist in the late 1940s, embarking on a life of Islamist writing and activism that has earned him stature of modern Egypt's most influential radical Islamist thinker. He was eventually imprisoned for his views, but continued to write until his execution by the Egyptian government in 1966. He is now regarded in Muslim circles as *shahid*, or martyr.

John Calvert is assistant professor of history at Creighton University in Omaha, Nebraska, where he teaches courses related to the history of the modern Middle East. He received his Ph.D. in 1994 from the Institute of Islamic Studies at McGill University, Montreal. Since then he has published several articles dealing with Islamist movements and thinkers, including Sayyid Qutb.

William Shepard retired in 1999 from his post as associate professor of religious studies at the University of Canterbury in Christchurch, New Zealand, where he had taught since 1978. He received his Ph.D. in the comparative study of religion from Harvard University in 1973 and taught at Cornell College in Mount Vernon, Iowa, from 1971 to 1978. His main area of research is modern Islamic thought. He has published two books, *The Faith of a Modern Muslim Intellectual: The Religious Aspects and Implications of the Writings of Ahmad Amin* (1982), and *Sayyid Qutb and Islamic Activism: A Translation and Critical Analysis of "Social Justice in Islam"* (1996), and numerous articles, including several on Sayyid Qutb.

⬡ Contents

Acknowledgments

Ibrahim M. Abdel Halim, past president of the Canterbury Muslim Association, provided considerable help with translation and explained many of the customs referred to in the book. Sawsan Mahmoud, Nasser Alsharif, and Raed Jamil also gave some help with the translation. Ann Quinn and Dorothy Zarifeh read the whole English text and made important suggestions on wording and style. Elizabeth Gill also read part of the text and made suggestions. We wish to express our appreciation to all of them.

✸ Author's Introduction

These are pictures of the life of the village as it was in the time of my childhood, a quarter of a century ago. I have not embellished them in any way. I have done no more than transfer them from the ledger of my memory to the page of my notebook.

A few of these pictures have now passed away and been replaced by new ones. In recording them here I have provided a kind of literary museum in which pages of our national life and modern history are preserved. In fact, most of these images are still quite alive, but well-off city people have hardly any conception of them, whether as things in real life or even as imaginary things. This recording of them will give the new generation a picture of what is good and what is bad in our nation's countryside. Perhaps they will have an opinion as to what should remain and what should be discarded.

Translators' Introduction

Sayyid Qutb's Career

Sayyid Qutb, the author of the autobiographical work translated here, is best known as a radical Islamic writer and activist. He was, in fact, executed by the Egyptian government in 1966 for these activities, and today he is usually referred to in Muslim circles as *shahid*, or martyr. His influence on activists and on Muslims generally, through both his writings and his example, has been enormous. He came to his Islamic activism relatively late, however.

For the first half of his adult life Qutb was a fairly prominent member of the secular intellectual and literary elite that flourished in Egypt during the period of the monarchy (1922–52) and included such figures as Taha Hussein and Naguib Mahfouz. Qutb was a poet and literary critic, as well as a writer on educational and social matters. Relatively little attention has been given to this period of his life, but it is interesting both in its own right and for the light it sheds on his later life. This book, *A Child from the Village*, was written only two or three years before Qutb turned to Islamist ideology, but no trace of that ideology appears in it. However, it does reveal some of Qutb's strong concern for social justice—concern he was presently to express in Islamic terms. Also, and perhaps more important, especially for those not interested in Qutb himself, this book gives the reader a remarkable look into the life of an Egyptian village nearly a century ago. We get almost a ringside seat at the introduction of modern-style schooling and medicine, as well as insight into a wide array of customs and some examples of how the village sought to defend itself against the intrusions of the central government and "modernity."

The village in question is Musha, which is located in Asyut Province, in Upper Egypt, somewhat more than two hundred miles south of Cairo. Sayyid Qutb was born there in September 1906, at a time when developments begun nearly a century before were in many areas just beginning to bear visible fruit.

Egypt was then slightly more than half-way through the period of British occupation, which had begun in 1882 and was to end in 1922. It had been about a century since Muhammad Ali, an Albanian officer from the Ottoman army, had taken over the government, filling the power vacuum left by the withdrawal of Napoleon's French army in 1801 after a three-year occupation that had effectively demolished the previous political order. Muhammad Ali came to be known as "the great modernizer"; it was during his forty-four-year rule that the processes variously referred to as modernization, Westernization and secularization began in a concerted and conscious way. It was also during his rule that Egypt became independent—de facto if not yet de jure—of Ottoman rule from Istanbul. Muhammad Ali's grandson and eventual successor, Isma'il, ostentatiously pushed modernization, initiating several projects including the building of the Suez Canal; unfortunately, his efforts also put the government in debt to European creditors, setting the stage for the British occupation. This occupation occurred after a revolt by Egyptian army officers under Ahmad 'Urabi. It was during the first decade of the twentieth century that Egyptians began to show significant signs of resistance against this occupation. The most dramatic event in this connection was the Dinshaway incident, in which several peasants were executed after a quarrel with British soldiers. This event, which galvanized opposition at all levels of society, took place in 1906, the year of Sayyid Qutb's birth.

In Egypt, as elsewhere, modernization was to revolutionize society, politically, economically, and socially, but in many areas it was only becoming fully visible about the time Qutb was born. Western-style journalism began in the decade of Qutb's birth as did political parties, one of which, the Nationalist Party under Mustafa Kamil, called quite vocally for the departure of the British. Reformers were beginning to call for the liberation of women, and two notable books calling for this emancipation had been published in 1899 and 1901. As for education, Western-style schools mainly for the elite had made a beginning, but a government report in 1899 stated that there were 7,735 students in such schools and about 180,000 in the old-style *katatib* (schools), which mainly taught reading, writing, and recitation of the Qur'an.[1] The first Western-style university was opened in Cairo in 1908, about a year after Qutb was born. A state school was opened in Musha not long before Sayyid Qutb was old enough to enter it, in 1912.

Modernization is commonly thought of as a good thing and in many respects it is, but it also has its problematic aspects. It brings material improvements and both material and social opportunities but it also leads to psychological, social, and cultural stresses. Moreover, it definitely has winners and losers. Teachers in the old-style *katatib* and practitioners of old-style folk medicine, for example, saw their livelihoods threatened, while those able and positioned to gain the skills to be teachers in the new-style schools and doctors of the new-style medicine, or to enter other developing professions, were among the "winners." Central government was also one of the "winners," because modern methods enabled it to extend its writ to the provinces and to all social levels to a degree inconceivable earlier. In fact, modernization, at least in its early phases, generally favored the wealthy and powerful over the poor and powerless, though there are exceptions. Modernization also produced its own social distinctions, since those belonging to the "modern" sector of society, known as *effendis*, followed a more or less Western lifestyle and wore Western-style clothes. It was a cultural gap of this sort in Iran that set the stage for the Islamic revolution of 1979.

Sayyid Qutb was born into the sort of family that was able to participate in and profit from the modernization of the country. It is worth noting that the last three presidents of Egypt—Abdul Nasser, Anwar al-Sadat, and Hosni Mubarak—came from the same sort of background. Qutb's father and mother both came from established and respected families in their village, though their financial position had weakened and his father was gradually selling off his land to cover his debts. Still, he was very much respected as a pious and educated man. He subscribed to a daily newspaper and had joined the Nationalist Party and was a member of its local committee. At the age of six Qutb was sent to the new state elementary school, the point at which *A Child from the Village* begins. There had been some debate in the family whether to send him to the state school or to the traditional school, or *kuttab*, but his mother saw the state school as the beginning of an education that would make him an *effendi* and able to restore the family fortunes, and her will prevailed. Although at his father's insistence he did attend the *kuttab* for a single day, his experiences there led him to value the state school all the more—he refers to it as the "sacred school." He also memorized the Qur'an and encouraged some of his friends to do so too; he then organized Qur'an reciting competitions with the *kuttab* boys in order to show that the state school students were not deficient in this area. His account of his childhood ends when, at about the age of fifteen, he was sent to Cairo to attend secondary school. This move had been delayed by the disruptions connected with the Revolution of 1919, which involved major demonstrations against British rule and in favor of the nationalist leader Saad Zaghlul. When the British departed in 1922,

Egypt became formally independent, with an elected parliament under King Fu'ad I, a descendent of Muhammad Ali. Fu'ad was succeeded by his son Farouk in 1936, an arrangement that continued until the Free Officers' coup in 1952.

In Cairo Qutb lived with an uncle who was a journalist. He completed his secondary education and then, from 1929 to 1933, attended Dar al-'Ulum, a teacher training institution whose program might be described as a half-way house between the traditional education of the thousand-year-old university of al-Azhar and the education offered by the modern university. He then joined the Ministry of Education, working as a teacher for six years and then in varying capacities as an official in the ministry until October, 1952. In his early days in Cairo he became a member of the Wafd, the party of and most closely identified with the cause of nationalism and parliamentary government. Later he shifted to another party, the Saadist, but from 1945 he belonged to no party, presumably out of disgust with the politics of the time. Probably through his uncle he came to know 'Abbas Mahmud al-'Aqqad, a journalist, man of letters, and one of the leading secular intellectuals of the period, and Qutb became his disciple for some time. Qutb published his first article in a literary journal in 1924 and went on over the next thirty years to publish more than 130 poems and nearly 500 articles generally in the realms of literary, social, and political criticism. Up to 1947 he published some nine books, including a book on the task of poetry in the present generation, a volume of his own poetry entitled *The Unknown Shore*, a collection of some of his articles about current writers, a more theoretical book on literary criticism, two novelettes and two literary studies of the Qur'an. One of the novelettes, *Thorns*, is generally considered to be autobiographical. It describes an ill-starred and unsuccessful engagement in which the man comes through as rather conservative and quite uncertain of himself. It may shed some light on why Qutb never married, something unusual in Muslim society.

He also contributed to a book, *The Four Specters*, containing personal reminiscences by himself, by his brother, Muhammad, and by his sisters, Amina and Hamida. The brother and both of the sisters were to become involved in the Islamic movement along with him.

His articles included a series in the 1930s defending al-'Aqqad and another series commenting on Taha Hussein's book, *The Future of Culture in Egypt*, perhaps the best-known defense of Westernization written during that period. In his comments, he agrees with Taha Hussein's basic presuppositions and many of his specific proposals, but rejects his contention that the Egyptian mentality is close to that of the West and asserts the importance of retaining and renewing Egyptian and Arab culture. In the early 1940s, he wrote regularly on social issues for a journal published by the Ministry of Social Affairs. In these works he showed concern for the moral problems of society and for the unequal distribution of wealth, but he was far from revolutionary and often found positive models in Western institutions and experience.

After the end of the Second World War, with the end of wartime censorship, Sayyid Qutb and many others in his circle began to speak out forcefully and passionately for full national independence and social justice against the continuing European imperialism and the political corruption, social stress, and economic inequality that would soon bring about the collapse of the old regime. It was during this period, in 1945 or 1946, that *A Child from the Village* was published. Although the main stated purpose is to acquaint city dwellers with what country life is like, the social reform concerns are very close to the surface. Qutb's strong opinions did not endear him to those in power, and his critique of the political establishment may be the reason why he was sent on a study tour to the United States from November 1948 to August 1950. It is variously claimed that he was sent on this tour to avoid being arrested for his views, to get him out of the way, and to expose him directly to the West in the hopes that this exposure would moderate his opinions. This last goal was definitely not realized, Qutb was impressed by American technology but appalled at what he considered the low moral and cultural state of its people. He returned to Egypt all the more set in the direction his life had begun to move.

This direction was toward Islamic activism. Before 1948 he had written almost nothing that could be called Islamist (that is, ideologically Islamic). Indeed, later on he was to describe himself as irreligious during this period. His literary studies of the Qur'an do not seem to be the work of an unbeliever but they certainly do not push an Islamist agenda. In 1948 he published several clearly Islamist articles in *New Thought*, a journal that he edited for a few months until it was closed down under martial law at the beginning of the Palestine war. More importantly, during this same year he wrote the first of his Islamist books, *Social Justice in Islam*, which was published just after he went to the United States. In these writings he makes many of the same demands for social justice that he made earlier, but they are given an Islamic foundation and he calls for a society governed by Islamic norms, though he evidently was still prepared to cooperate with people of a more secularist orientation for common social and political goals. As far as we can discover, it is not known specifically why he turned to Islamism at this point, though one may surmise that the war in Palestine had an effect.

Soon after his return to Egypt from the United States, possibly as early as 1951 and certainly by 1953, he joined the Muslim Brothers, an organization with a very large following calling for Islamic moral reform and the implementation of Islamic laws. This organization had been founded in 1928 and by the late 1940s and early 1950s was a serious contender for political power. Qutb soon became one of its leading ideologues, writing articles in its journals and editing one of them for a time in 1954. By 1954, his book *Social Justice in Islam* had gone through four editions, and he had written two shorter books,

Islam and World Peace (1951) and *Islam's Battle with Capitalism* (1951). He also had begun his commentary on the Qur'an, *In the Shade of the Qur'an*, which he was to continue working on for the rest of his life. He supported the Free Officers coup in 1952, as did the Muslim Brothers, and he appears to have sat in the inner councils of the Free Officers for a few months, but left when he realized that they were not prepared to institute the Islamist program for society that the Brothers stood for. He also resigned from the Ministry of Education in October 1952 and criticized its policies. During this period, he continued to write articles for secular journals, some but not all explicitly Islamist in content. He ceased writing poetry.

The Muslim Brothers increasingly fell out with the government and, after an attempt on the life of Abdul Nasser in October 1954, the government banned the organization, executing some of its leaders and imprisoning many others. Qutb was among the latter: he spent most of the rest of his life in prison, mainly in the prison hospital because of ill health. From prison he continued to write and to revise earlier writings, and his writing became more and more radically Islamist. It is generally assumed that the harsh conditions and torture that he and others suffered contributed in a major way to this radicalism. A particularly serious episode occurred in 1957, when prison guards killed more than twenty of the Muslim Brothers and injured many more; Qutb's most radical works appear to date from after this event. He was released from prison toward the end of 1964 but rearrested a few months later, accused of plotting against the government. By this time he had come to an extremely radical Islamist position that left no room for cooperation with secularists. His primary emphasis was less on social reform as such than on doing the will of God as expressed in the authoritative writings of Islam, whatever the cost. He openly declared that the existing order in all countries, including so-called Muslim ones, was anti-Islamic, indeed *jahili* (that is, barbaric and ignorant), and he called on Islamic activists to prepare themselves to replace it. His book *Milestones*, which was published during his brief period of freedom and expressed these views quite forcefully, was one of the main pieces of evidence against him at his trial. He was convicted and was executed on August 29, 1966.

His writings after his arrest were all Islamist, and he is said to have disowned his pre-Islamist works. Two more editions of *Social Justice in Islam*, considerably modified to reflect his later views, were published in 1958 and 1964. After *In the Shade of the Qur'an* was completed, Qutb began to revise it, completing the new commentary to slightly less than half of the Qur'an before his death. Other books include *This Religion* (1961), *The Future Belongs to This Religion* (1962?), *Islam and the Problems of Civilization* (1962), *Characteristics of the Islamic Conception* (1962), *Milestones* (1964, already mentioned), and *Components of the Islamic Conception* (published posthumously). A number of his articles have been collected and published as books since his death.

Today Qutb is known mainly as an Islamist ideologue and martyr and is considered to have provided major inspiration for diverse radical Islamist movements since his death. His earlier career is not forgotten, however. Most of his pre-Islamist books, including *A Child from the Village*, are in print and are read. A collection of all of his known poems (more than half not in his collection *The Unknown Shore*) was published in Egypt in 1989. The earlier as well as the later Qutb lives on.

A Village Childhood

Constituting a little more than two hundred pages in its various Arabic editions, *A Child from the Village* is divided into twelve chapters, each bearing a title suggestive of its content. Befitting a man who considered himself a litterateur, the book's prose style is sophisticated and its vocabulary rich and evocative. In places, particularly in its "thick description" of Musha's cultural beliefs and practices, the book's tone is almost anthropological, evidence of the degree to which Qutb as an adult had distanced himself from the parochial outlook of his village background. Qutb reinforces this sense of cultural estrangement by referring to himself throughout the book in the third person, thus allowing the reader easily to distinguish between the author's adult worldview and that of his child protagonist. He treats his life between roughly the ages of six and fifteen but his narrative lacks a distinct chronological thread. Rather, he presents his material in a series of episodes, which, despite their anecdotal nature, are highly developed and thematic in character. Taken together, these vignettes document what Qutb perceived to be his "awakening" from the unreflective slumber of customary rural life to a new kind of existence lived within the problematic context of the modernizing nation-state. In relating his story, Qutb knows that he is addressing other Egyptians who had made similar journeys from rural villages to Cairo in order to partake of that city's larger and more complex social reality.

Qutb's autobiography is one of a number of autobiographical works written by Egyptian authors in the early and middle decades of the twentieth century. Within this cluster of works, pride of place belongs to *al-Ayyam* (volume 1, 1929; volume 2, 1939; volume 3, 1973) by Taha Hussein (1889–1973), which relates the author's years growing up in a rural community in Upper Egypt and his efforts to transcend the limitations of village life by means of modern education. Especially in the first volume, Taha Hussein casts a critical eye on features of Egypt's social and intellectual life that he believed hindered Egypt's transition to modernity, including the folk beliefs of the villagers and the spiritual and social authority held by the tradition-minded men of religion. Implicit in Hussein's autobiography is the idea that these and other manifestations of tradition must be jettisoned from the national culture if Egypt is to take its place among the progressive nations of the world.

Al-Ayyam's significance derives in large measure from its status as
the first truly modern autobiography in the Arabic language. As articles in a recent edited study have shown, self-narrative has a long
pedigree within Islam's literary culture.[2] However, prior to the twentieth century literary self-portrayal tended to focus on the author's
role as transmitter of religious knowledge or on the development of
his inner person, with little reference to his cultural and material environment. On occasion, the purpose of this kind of work was also
doctrinal, as in the case of the polemical *Deliverance from Error* by the
religious scholar Abu Hamid al-Ghazali (1058–1111), in which the
author upheld the superiority of Sufism over other types of religious
expression. In contrast to these early examples of autobiography, *al-
Ayyam* displays a distinctly secular sensibility, in which the consciousness of its protagonist is viewed as developing in time and
within a variety of social, economic, and cultural contexts.

Al-Ayyam's prominence as a literary text encouraged several writers, including Qutb, to choose autobiography as a vehicle for re-
counting their oftentimes similar encounters with the forces of
change. Like *al-Ayyam*, Qutb's autobiography documents its youthful
protagonist's acquisition of new knowledge and perspectives. In fact,
Qutb explicitly acknowledged his debt to Taha Hussein in the dedi-
catory inscription at the beginning of *A Child from the Village*, the translation of which is provided in the present work. However, despite
this similarity between the two books, the purpose of the two authors
is somewhat different. Whereas Taha Hussein was led by his experiences to embrace the civilization of the West, Sayyid Qutb's response
was to seek a modernized and reformed version of the Egyptian national community, which, throughout his career as a writer, he identified with Eastern, Muslim civilization. Other writers who took cues
from al-Ayyam include Ibrahim al-Mazini (*Qissat Hayah*, 1943),
Salama Musa (*Tarbiyat Salama Musa*, 1947), Ahmad Amin (*Hayati*,
1950, revised 1952), Ibrahim 'Abd al-Halim (*Ayyam al-Tufula*, 1953),

and Tawfiq al-Hakim (*Sijn al-'Umr*, 1964). Although each of the auto-biographical works of these authors brings to bear its own particular perspective, all tend to treat their subjects as moving from early states of ignorance to higher levels of critical social and personal awareness. In documenting such individual journeys, these books are in large degree concerned with Egypt's effort to create itself as a modern nation.

Judging from Qutb's descriptions in *A Child from the Village*, Musha was fairly typical of the villages and small towns that dotted the floodplain of southern Egypt. He describes Musha as a community of agrarian producers with a sprinkling of traders and petty merchants, and presumably many of these were also farmers. In Qutb's day the livelihood of the region's peasant inhabitants still largely depended on the effects of the annual inundation of the Nile, which flooded the fields in late summer to lay down a fertile layer of rich black earth. In one passage, Qutb explains how the season of "wet planting" was followed by the busy time of the harvest, when migrant workers from less privileged villages and provinces would arrive in the village to help out. The tombs and burial grounds that mark the cliff faces and barren plains of Asyut Province and elsewhere in the valley bear mute testimony to the myriad farming communities that had taken advantage of this fecundity since Neolithic times.

However, changes were already under way during Qutb's childhood that would eventually utterly transform this natural cycle. Continuing the efforts of Muhammad Ali and the Khedive Isma'il, the British administration worked to replace the traditional system of basin irrigation, which captured and held the floodwaters by means of levees and dykes, with a perennial system not dependent on the seasonal inundation. This process of controlling the flood eventually culminated in the construction of the Aswan Dam by Egyptian president Abdul Nasser. The last inundation of the Nile occurred in 1965, one year before Qutb's death. However, during the period the autobiography is set, the overall effects of these changes were still in the future. Qutb writes in his autobiography of how the village was transformed during the flood into a series of islands. He remembers that he and his boyhood companions would playfully jump into the waters from the rooftop of their school.

According to Qutb, the village was a reasonably prosperous place, at least when compared with neighboring villages. Each family, we learn, owned a house, "whether large or small," and the land was fairly evenly divided among the different families. The village stood nearby a Coptic monastery, which had been prominent enough in its medieval heyday to merit a mention in the great topographical survey of the fifteenth-century historian Taqi al-Din al Maqrizi (d. 1442). Qutb does not say so, but the monastery would have been a tangible reminder for Musha's Muslim populace that even after centuries of indigenous conversion and Arab-Muslim settlement, Coptic Christians, with whom Muslims shared much in the way of culture, continued to comprise a significant portion of southern Egypt's population.

As in other village communities, the communal identity of Musha's Muslim inhabitants was largely shaped by religion. Especially important were the weekly congregational prayers, feast days, and, above all, the tomb of Musha's Muslim saint (*wali*), identified in *A Child from the Village* as Shaykh 'Abd al-Fattah, which served as the focus of popular religious devotion and festivities, including the practice of praying for the saint's intercession with God for the bestowal of favors and blessings. Although the tomb is not described in the book, we may picture it as more or less identical to saints' tombs elsewhere in Egypt—a simple square structure capped by a dome. Once a year, Musha, like other Egyptian villages, would have came alive in raucous celebration of the *mawlid*, the commemoration of the saint's passing from the earthly realm.

Qutb recounts other expressions of popular religion and belief. He relates, for example, how within every villager's mind, including his own, there existed an unshakable belief in a parallel reality of unseen, mainly malign forces. These were the jinn and the *'afarit*, which hovered over the lives of the people like ominous clouds. According to Qutb, they could be expected to manifest anywhere, at any time and in a variety of forms, including the shape of a black cat, dozens of which roamed the dark and twisted pathways of the village at night. When Qutb's baby brother died of tetanus seven days after birth, the result of the midwife's infected surgical knife, the family was quick to blame the death on the baby's invisible "twin," the ghostly companion that the villagers believed haunted the lives of every child and adult. According to Qutb, these intrusive elements could be managed only by the evocation of the saints (*awliya*) or the opportune recitation of a Qur'anic verse. Qutb tells us that after his baby brother's death he was given an amulet with a depiction of the Prophet Solomon to wear as protection against Iblis and his demonic offspring. He mentions in passing how the women of the village would conduct *zar* ceremonies, exorcisms characterized by trance-like music and dancing to ward off the negative effects of demonic possession. At the very beginning of the book he introduces his readers to the fearsome figure of the "God-possessed" Magzub, whose disheveled appearance and unconventional behavior were considered by the adults of the village to be signs of divine favor, although for Qutb and his young companions the Magzub was a terrifying figure to be avoided.

Qutb tells us that in time he came to dismiss the *'afarit* and magic of the supernatural world as figments of the popular imagination. Here he cites the influence of one of his teachers at the state school, who sought hard to prove to his students that the phenomena they attributed to occult forces had natural explanations. Qutb goes on to say, however, that although his belief in supernatural phenomena dissipated over time, they "were more deeply embedded in his soul than education and that the *'afarit* of his childhood and youth continued to inhabit his adult imagination" as the imprint of his rural upbringing.

Here Qutb touches on a theme found throughout the body of his writings, namely, that Egyptians such as himself are possessed of an inherent spiritual sensibility that distinguished them from the essentially materialistic outlook of the West. As Qutb was coming to appreciate around the time he wrote his autobiography, this spiritual outlook, manifested vulgarly in village beliefs, was perfectly expressed in adherence to the divinely ordained principles of the Qur'an.

There was another, more formal and learned expression of religion in Musha. Qutb writes that amid a village population that was largely illiterate he was eager to tap into the knowledge and social power that came with the study of Islam's scholarly tradition. Role models of scholarly achievement existed within his extended family; we learn that two of his maternal uncles had as young men attended the Azhar, and that their studies there had transformed them into figures of local prestige. Qutb relates that from an early age he attempted to broaden his understanding of Islamic doctrine by attending lessons in Qur'anic interpretation provided by students of the Azhar who visited villages like Musha on holidays as a service to provincial Egyptians. The lessons were related in the difficult, elevated discourse of formal literary Arabic, which differed on points of grammar and vocabulary from the earthy dialect of everyday conversation. It was largely through the lessons imparted by these scholars that Qutb was introduced to what the anthropologist Robert Redfield termed the "Great Tradition" of texts and theological schools, which differed from the "Little Tradition" of the largely non-literate rural population. This background enabled Qutb to enter the school system in Cairo with an appreciation of the classical texts of Islam that was enthusiastic and relatively well formed. It is worthwhile to note that the Islam described by Qutb in his autobiography, whether of the folk or scholarly variety, differed substantially from his maturing Islamist discourse. In contrast to the devotional practices and beliefs of traditional individual and community-oriented piety, Islamist discourse interprets Islam as ideology in support of political and social activism.

Group identity in this rural setting was also determined by patrilineal kinship ties, which defined family units in relation to the other social collectivities with which they had contact, including those of village and neighborhood. Family relationships were strengthened by the limited availability within the village of natural and social resources, which sometimes made them the sources of inter-familial contention. A challenge from within the village to a family's social or material standing could, and often did, lead to the outbreak of feuding, which normally ended with the shedding of blood or the payment of a compensatory fee by the offending party. Qutb's extended family did not escape involvement in this form of local justice. In his autobiography, he recalls how assailants exacted revenge upon one of his uncles by poisoning and mutilating his cattle. Even today southern Egypt has a reputation among Egyptians for its relatively high incidence of vendetta killings.

Yet, despite the occurrence of intercommunal strife, the demanding material conditions of village life required that the inhabitants of Musha establish ties of social solidarity. As Father Henri Habbib Aryout remarked in his 1933 classic *The Egyptian Peasant*, "When the vital interests of a village are threatened, everyone feels deeply that he is one of the community: Men, women, children all grouped together in a single force."[3] Such a threat, Qutb tells us, occurred when fire broke out in the home of one of the villagers, a *shaykh* whose holiness attracted the sick and infirm of the village. Concern for the *shaykh* and fear that the fire might spread quickly among the stalks of corn and cotton that were stored on the roofs of the houses prompted the villagers to mobilize and douse the fire with water skins. Qutb goes on to explain how, in the aftermath of the tragedy, the villagers stood by their *shaykh* when his holy powers were put to question by an official medical doctor who came from the city to investigate a death caused by the fire. In this and other ways, the villagers closed ranks against the intrusion of an outsider.

Even Musha's thieves operated according to an ethic that looked to the overall well-being of the community. In Qutb's account, thieves who robbed the weak were despised and those who robbed the rich and powerful were admired. Consequently, the village mainstream tended to delight in the "adventures" of the thieves, viewing them as a means of restoring the social balance that the rich, through their alleged avarice, were believed to have upset.

In the face of these strong familial and village ties, it is not surprising that membership in administrative units such as Asyut Province or the much larger Egyptian nation-state did not normally register in the consciousness of Musha's inhabitants as meaningful or significant. If the villagers identified in supravillage terms at all, it was only vaguely and then as members of the *umma*, the worldwide community of Muslims.

Yet here, too, things were beginning to change. Qutb recounts how the parochial vision of local community was gradually replaced by a new, encompassing national vision, which began to form as a result of patriotic sentiments that developed in the country during World War I and its aftermath. By the time Qutb had reached school age, demands for the end of the British occupation had become commonplace among Egyptians, especially educated men like his father. Qutb remembers how supporters of the Nationalist Party would meet at the family home to discuss politics and the Egyptian-Ottoman resistance to Britain and its wartime allies, symbolized by the popular Egyptian ruler, the exiled Khedive 'Abbas II. Influences such as this enabled the young Qutb to acquire a sense of national belonging beyond the limited world of his kinship and village identities. He writes that he found an outlet for his emergent nationalism in the uprising of 1919, sparked by Britain's exile of Saad Zaghlul, the leader of the

"Egyptian Delegation" (al-Wafd al-Misri), which lobbied for Egypt's independence after the war. Encouraged by one of his schoolteachers, he composed naïve though heartfelt patriotic speeches and poems, which he delivered "in meeting halls and mosques, where the spirit of the revolution was breathed into all." Qutb's autobiography gives us a rare glimpse of the mood surrounding the uprising at the village level.

As mentioned, Qutb infuses his personalized account of tradition and modernization in a rural community with a strong social justice message. Despite its tone of nostalgia, *A Child from the Village* paints a picture of the Egyptian countryside that is not entirely happy. The specter of peasant indebtedness and loss of land haunts the pages of the autobiography, as does disease caused by unhygienic conditions and the peasants' recourse to folk remedies and barber-surgeons rather than scientifically trained physicians. The joys of Ramadan, birth ceremonies, and other festive occasions are juxtaposed to death, tragedy, and the laments of women whose families patiently endure hard lives. Captives of poverty and ignorance, the peasants of Qutb's autobiography toil endlessly in their fields with little expectation that their lives will improve. They are the victims of the few large landowners and politicians who controlled Egypt's wealth. According to Tetz Rooke, who examined a wide range of Arabic childhood autobiographies, the critical portrayal of rural life found *A Child from the Village* represents a "break with the tendency towards pastoral idealization which dominated much of the first Egyptian creative writing concerned with country life." It may thus be seen as a "precursor of the later Egyptian novel that embraces the subject of the village with a true-to-life, descriptive intent such as *al-Ard* [The earth, 1953] by 'Abd al-Rahman al-Sharqawi (1920–1987)."[4] In the context of the mid-1940s, Qutb's book manifests a growing awareness among Egypt's intelligentsia of socioeconomic issues. It was during this period, for example, that dissident elements within the Wafd founded the Wafdist Vanguard in order to influence the party leadership in a leftist direction.

Implicitly and sometimes explicitly in the book, Qutb advocates the need for reform and modernization at the village level. Qutb believed that the introduction of modern schooling in Musha was a step in the right direction, but he also believed that there was need for many more improvements, especially in the areas of land reform and health care. In his view, the Egyptian government was the obvious agent to undertake the necessary reforms, but too often the state's ameliorative efforts were imposed with a heavy hand or else were ill conceived. Qutb provides a harrowing account of a government operation, probably staged shortly after World War I, to confiscate all weapons belonging to the villagers of Asyut Province as a precondition for its integration into the structure of the State on a more thorough basis. He describes how soldiers, having surrounded the village, brutally interrogated the peasants, at one point firing bullets over the heads of the assembled village elders. Events such as this reinforced the peasants' traditional distrust of a governmental authority that in the past periodically subjected them to corvée labor. Elsewhere in the book, Qutb documents, sometimes with humor, the unwelcome and often inexpert intrusions of various government officials into the affairs of the community. We are introduced to medical officials, coroners, judges, and others, all of whom attempt to order and police the countryside in ways that make sense to the State but not to the villagers. In much the same way as the Egyptian writer Tawfiq al-Hakim's novella *Diary of a Country Prosecutor*, *A Child from the Village* documents the gulf in understanding that existed between urban officialdom and the dwellers of the countryside, the difference being that in Qutb's book we are provided with the perspective of the peasants rather than that of a government official. Qutb appears to argue that if modernization in Egypt's countryside is to be effective, it must take into account the sensibilities and social and economic realities of its inhabitants.

Within two years of the publication of *A Child from the Village*, Qutb adopted the Islamist position upon which his fame rests. Whatever the exact reasons for his ideological change, the significant point is that Qutb's early Islamist writings display many of the same basic concerns for social justice and national community that figure in his secular writings, including *A Child from the Village*. A discussion of the ways in which Qutb grafted the symbols and doctrines of the Qur'an is beyond the scope of this introduction. What can be said is that *A Child from the Village* illuminates an important element of the context out of which Qutb's Islamism emerged.

A CHILD FROM THE VILLAGE

1   The *Magzub*

More than a quarter-century has passed since these events, but even today he cannot recall them without feeling in his body a shudder that silently penetrates his bones, as if his blood had turned to ice water. It was this man with disheveled hair and torn clothing, sometimes naked with nothing to cover his body, wandering about the streets and alleys of the village with a stick in his hand that struck at everything and everybody. He would let out a confused but terrifying growl or guffaw in a high, dreadful voice.

The boy was less than six years old when people in the village began to whisper about Shaykh Naqib, and he heard them say that he had taken "the medicine" and that it was going hard with him. "The medicine"? He knew all too well what medicine was. He still remembers that one day he came down with a fever, and they made him swallow that bitter, foul-tasting, and foul-smelling liquid, using all sorts of inducements and threats. Then nature took its course! But how could "the medicine" turn this man, Shaykh Naqib, into a fearsome wandering devil, out of his mind, staring blankly and behaving so strangely? What "medicine" was this that could turn people into zombies?

The man used to tear his clothes to shreds and then roll in the mud or pour dust over his head and naked body, until the dust and mud coating his skin formed a new set of clothes, replacing the torn and discarded ones. He used to run through the streets of the village screaming in a shrill, terrifying voice, "Allah! Allah! Allah!" or shuffle along slowly, growling and muttering, "Ee! Ee! Ee!" Or he would puff up his chest with air, alternately bowing down and standing erect, reciting, *"Hayy! Hayy! Hayy!"*[1] Also, he would often take shelter by a stone bench or a pillar and crouch there in silence, huddled up like a drug addict, not moving a muscle or batting an eyelash. At times he would stay that way for hours on end.

What connection could a small child see between medicine and all of this? Later he learned that this was the "medicine of saint-hood"(!) and that the great *awliya*[2] met yearly on Mount Qaf with the Qutb al-Ghawth presiding.[3] Then they observed the condition of the world and decided its fate as they willed. He also learned that one of the things they decided was the distribution of "medicine" to those elect servants of God whom they chose. Sometimes the blow would strike a pleasant and mild-mannered man, and sometimes a rough and violent man. In both cases it would turn him into a *magzub*,[4] but in the first case his medicine would be mild, his period of abstraction would be easy, and he would proceed peacefully on to the level of saintship. For the other person, however, the medicine would be harsh and he would suffer severely during the period until his soul was cleansed, his spirit purified, and his nature softened. Only then would he pass on to the next stage and become calm and peaceful.

He also heard another explanation for the severity or ease of the medicine. Ease or turmoil resulted from the amount of "medicine." Sometimes it was a large dose and caused the person who took it effort and turmoil because it was more than he could bear, so that its violent and inebriating effects would stay with him for a long time, rending his body and deranging his mind. But when God finally ordained his return to health, he had a high place in the scale of saints. Sometimes the dose was small and the person did not have much effort or difficulty in taking it, and the period of abstraction lasted only as long as it took the medicine to settle into his system. Then he was a saint, but much lower in the scale.

But a thousand and one explanations could not put the small child's heart at rest. There had been times when he was walking alone or with his companions and Shaykh Naqib suddenly appeared, they knew not from where. What he knew was that their mouths went dry and their feet froze to the ground when he appeared at the end of the road, even if he were dozens of meters away from them. Their legs became paralyzed, their eyes stared at him without blinking, their hearts beat violently but they could not move a muscle. They had been like a poor bird mesmerized by a snake, realizing that it is about to be caught but unable to fly away, or like the mouse that the cat plays with before it pounces for the kill. For they knew there was no use trying to escape. The *shaykh* could "stride," and when they asked for an explanation of this they were given to understand that he transported himself every Friday from their village to the Ka'ba, performed the congregational prayer with the *awliya* and the righteous ones, and then returned. They had heard a lot about how long and difficult a journey the hajj was.[5] In those days it meant riding on the back of a camel after crossing the Red Sea. And here the *shaykh* could make the whole long trip in a single step—one step to go and another to come back.

What use to try and run away when he could immediately have them in his reach again? They had heard that the terrible stick that the *shaykh* had in his hand could lengthen or shorten as he wished and indeed that his hand could reach anything near or far whenever he wished.

So what use to try and run away? That stick could burn their backs or break their ribs, and the man would not even have to move from his place to chase them. Certainly not. Indeed, they had heard that he could "nail" them to the spot where they were. And had he not "nailed" a rebellious demon that was terrifying the people in one of the streets of the village? The *'ifrit*[6] remained "nailed" until dawn. It pleaded with the *shaykh* for his help and protection, and apologized and begged for pardon, and promised that it would leave the village entirely and not expose the people to its evil any more. Still, the *shaykh* did not release it until he had exacted solemn and strict promises and threatened it with a dire fate if it should go back on them. From that day the *'ifrit* never again appeared in that place.

Were they stronger and faster than *'afarit*?

No use! No use!

But their hearts almost stopped, their bones turned to water, and their mouths dried up so that they could not even move their tongues. They swallowed what saliva they could to relieve the dryness of their throats while their eyes stared at this fearsome and terrifying man. Then he began to move . . .

Either he would turn off into one of the many winding streets of the village before he reached them, in which case they would breathe a sigh of relief and, gathering what remained of their strength, run like the wind, panting with deadly fright; or he would come up to them and they would huddle together like chicks attacked by a predatory cat or a weasel. Then they would approach him in a flattering way, asking to kiss his hand, their eyes staring at the fearsome stick in his hand. Sometimes they would come out of this contact safe and sound, but other times they would taste its "sweet" fruit.

How often they had heard from the older people that this stick came from a tree in paradise, though all they saw was a piece of a common palm branch, or that it had been dipped seven times in the Well of Zamzam[7] and that the person who received a blow from it was extremely blessed. It would only touch an afflicted, or diseased, part of the body—even though the person might be unaware of the disease—and one had only to come into contact with the stick to be cured.

They used to see some men come up to the *shaykh* in the road and jostle against him, if he was calm, until he got stirred up. The aim was to receive blows from that stick mainly on their backs, while they sought to protect their faces and heads. Then they would go away content, hiding the pain they felt and insisting that the stick felt like an angel of bliss. As for the children, they knew quite well what this heavenly angel felt like. Their backs shrank under the blows of that accursed stick and they tried to dissemble as the men did but they couldn't. Moreover, the very demeanor of the man, his glances, his voice, his movements, were guaranteed to arouse fear in their hearts even before he touched them.

The boy marveled at something else, besides the men's claim that the stick was pleasant and soft. The *magzub* spent most of his time naked and the hair of his body and head was matted and hardened like the hide of an elephant, yet men or women showed no visible shame or embarrassment when they saw this naked and filthy body. Whenever he would ask about this, he would be told, "Be quiet. He is no longer an ordinary person; he is no longer subject to the rules of society. He has been endowed with sainthood and no longer belongs to the earthly realm in which we live."

Then the boy had an accident. While playing a game that involved twisting his body and bending his neck, he had contorted his neck in such a way that if he wanted to look in a particular direction he had to move his whole body, in much the same manner as a hyena. This condition continued for a long time and the symptoms got worse, and his family began to worry about him because this malady seemed to go on forever. At first his friends pitied him, but then they began to wink at each other and mimic his odd posture when he wasn't looking, and finally to laugh openly. He wanted a cure for this painful malady at any cost.

Then one of the women came and saw him and said to his mother, "Woman, do you leave your child like that?"

She said, in great distress, "What can we do? We have tried everything and nothing works."

The woman said, "I'll show you the only solution."

The worried mother looked at her, and so did he. She said, "Leave him for a night with Shaykh Naqib!"

The mother did not understand—nor did he at first—but the woman made herself perfectly clear, saying: "One of the family must follow the *shaykh* to find out where he sleeps and must put the boy beside him and leave him there until morning, and he will wake up cured."

"What?"

His hair stood on end and his body turned to gooseflesh at this terrifying suggestion. He should spend a whole night with that strange man? Why not then send him to the snake pit or the lion's den? Indeed, why not put him face-to-face with the devil? Or was it he who was crazy? Although he did not believe for one instant that the woman seriously meant what she said, he cannot remember any terror that so penetrated his whole being throughout the rest of his life as this one did when he heard that sick joke. Although he felt quite confident that this suggestion would not be carried out, even if they used many more enticements and threats than they used to get him to take the medicine, his gaze still fastened on his mother's lips, as if he were awaiting a death sentence or an acquittal. He swallowed hard and took a slow deep breath, as his mother said, "No. No. Am I so crazy that I would make my son spend a night with the *magzub*? We will leave the matter to the knowledge and power of God."

What a blessing and relief! But he still remembers that moment and cannot forget it even after so many years.

2   The Gym Master

The child grew up in a family that did not have great wealth but did have prestige. It had once possessed great wealth, but this had been divided up and diminished by the process of inheritance. His father still had a reasonable portion, but it was never enough. He had become the head of the family and as such was obliged to keep up its name and position, even though with his limited share of the inheritance he could hardly afford what the family wealth as a whole had previously allowed. In the countryside, however, he dared not be seen to fail to keep up all his obligations. He was, furthermore, lavish in his hospitality and that increased the burden on his wealth. But to the last moment he kept up all appearances and met all expectations.

His mother's family was equally old and respected, or more so. Exactly the same thing had happened to her family as to his, but its standing was increased by the fact that two of her brothers had been sent to the Azhar in Cairo,[1] as usually happened with boys from wealthy rural families, and this gave the family a kind of scholarly stature alongside its regular rural prestige. In addition to all this, his maternal grandfather had spent a large part of his life in Cairo, along with his wife, and when he returned to the village he built a house that was as much like the houses of the capital as possible in its design, its decoration, its standards of quality, and its adherence to accepted conventions, because he had enough money to achieve what

7

he wanted. This was the environment the boy grew up in, and everything around him made him feel as if he belonged in some place other than the village.

When he reached the age of six, his family considered that it was time for him to start his schooling, but their opinions were divided. One group wanted him to go to the *kuttab*[2] to memorize the Qur'an and to obtain the *baraka*[3] that comes from having the Book of God by heart. The other group wanted him to go to the state primary school because it was cleaner and more progressive, and the Qur'an was taught there also, along with other subjects. The debate swirled on about him and he did not even know it. Finally the partisans of the school won out and the decision was made. He was informed of the decision and agreed, but without any evident enthusiasm, for he would rather have stayed at home playing with his sister, who was a little older than he, or playing in the street with the other children his age.

He was a bit spoiled because he was his parents' only boy, with an older sister and a younger sister, so he had not gotten used to the normal inconveniences of life that he would not be able to avoid once in school. In particular, he heard people say that the *kuttab* "pinched" the children, that is, weakened their health and stunted their growth. As for the school, he had heard something else that did not in general make him feel at ease about it.

Not many days passed before he was made ready for school. They brought him a *tarbush* (fez) in place of the *taqiya* (skullcap) he was used to wearing. They bought him a new pair of shoes in place of his old worn ones. They had a small *quftan* made from wool in place of his *gallabiyya*.[4] It was unusual to get such new clothes for school. It was done to entice and bribe him to go. All this had a decisive effect on his attitude toward the school, because the school was the cause of all this special treatment.

On the first morning his father and a friend of his took him to school. Now there is a story about this school.

The *katatib* had been the only houses of learning in the village until the provincial council opened this school and appointed a *faqih*[5] and an *'arif* to teach in it. Now the *faqih* was from a neighboring town. He had memorized the Qur'an as the Qur'an reciters do and then had attended government-organized classes in mathematics, general knowledge, and rudiments of educational methods. Then he was appointed *faqih* at the school. The *'arif* was one of the people in the village who had memorized the Qur'an and also ran its *kuttab*. The council had appointed him *'arif* until such time as the colleges for primary teachers should graduate enough people to take the places of *faqihs* and *'arifs*.

This *'arif* was highly trusted by the villagers, for it was his father who had taught their elders in his *kuttab*. He was known as a model of severity and sincerity. It was especially his severity with the children that made their parents trust him. When his father died, he and his brother had taken over the *kuttab*, running it just as their father had, until he was chosen to teach at the school and given a salary of a hundred and fifty piastres. He turned over the work of the *kuttab* entirely to his brother, while he went to the school so as to get what he earned from it as well as what came in from the *kuttab*, even though the latter lost a few students who were attracted to the school by its novelty.

The school did not really have any effect on the *katatib*, because the only ones who went to the school were the ones who had failed to memorize the Qur'an and had reached the age of puberty or beyond. When the school opened, their families sent them there or else they went on their own, mostly to have a good time, or in the faint hope of a second chance.

Because the school initially needed to win the confidence of the families and the students, it followed a most extraordinary system for determining which classes the students would be in. The level of the student's actual knowledge and understanding was not what determined which class was appropriate, but rather the student's age. Thus the tall boys were most likely to be in the fourth year, especially if their mustaches had begun to grow. Then came those smaller than they in the third year, and so on to the children in the kindergarten, which prepared them for the first year. But this principle was not always followed, for the children of the prominent village families took their places in the higher classes even though their age or height did not dictate this. It was not uncommon for a father to come and complain that his son had been put in the first year while so-and-so's son was in the second year, though he had no less status and wealth than that person. His request would be immediately accepted and the boy would be transferred to the year requested so as not to offend the family's honor.

According to these principles, our boy had to be put in the fourth year from the first day, especially as his cousin was in that class. It seemed right to seat them together so that his cousin could keep him company. But the director of the school saw that the child's father had some degree of culture and understanding and decided to speak with him frankly and explain to him that it was in the child's interest to begin in the kindergarten with the other children of his age and so progress in the normal way. He convinced him, and the child was handed over to the *faqih* and to the *'arif*, who was well known to him, because it was he who recited the Qur'an in their house during the month of Ramadan.

The father and his friend went their way after delivering him to the school with the necessary "recommendation," a recommendation whose effect he saw in the joy on the face of the *faqih* and the solicitous care, indeed pampering, he received from the *'arif*.

The father and his friend went their way only to return just before ten o'clock with pastry and sweets that his mother had carefully prepared, for the whole household on that day was in a tizzy of anticipation as if something unprecedented were happening. But when they came they could not find him in the school or anywhere else. The reason for this had to do with the gym master.

And now I must tell another story, about the gym master.

The provincial council had to follow the principles of education precisely in its schools. And because athletics was a required part of education, the students had to participate in it, but neither the *faqih* nor the *'arif* knew anything about athletics. So the school board found an inspired solution, to appoint a retired soldier as instructor of athletics in all the schools under its jurisdiction. This "master," as he was called, was supposed to make the rounds of the schools in the scattered villages of the province over the course of the year, but he might happen to visit a given school once a year, or might not visit it at all.

Now the child's village was the most progressive of those in its vicinity and had a number of families well known for their hospitality. When he came to the village this "master" would get a wonderful reception from the people and find generous hospitality throughout the day, simply because he was a "master" and came from the district capital. Thus the day when he was in the village would be a very special day marked by special activity. This led him to repeat his visit to the school two or three times a year!

There were set movements that he taught the students. These were *saghadun,* or "right face," *soladun,* or "left face," *marsh,* or "forward march," then *bir,* or "raise the hands to chest level," and *bik,* or "raise the hands up high," and *itsh,* or "lower the hands to the sides."[6] This was called the first exercise, and there were three well-known "Swedish" exercises, which were performed using the same set of commands.

And woe betide the student who made an error in any of these movements. The bamboo cane in the officer's hand would burn into his back and sides. Then these country children would imagine him as the Devil, with his quick movements, lightning leaps, and extraordinarily precise way of doing the gymnastics, along with his yelling and scowling at them and his stick that he used to shake threateningly at them. All this caused such an overwhelming fear that each day that he was to come seemed like the Day of Judgment, whose terror turned the children's hair white. Our child heard so much from his older cousin about this devil—the gym master—that what he heard was one of the many things that made him uneasy about the school in spite of all its attractions.

Ill luck had it that his first day in school happened to be the day of this "trickster." What he had heard earlier was already enough to strike fear into his small heart, but those devilish students took advantage of his youth and inexperience to terrify him with exaggerated stories that were more than he could stand. They said that this master would not only hit those who failed to perform the difficult and complicated movements, but would also hang them by their legs from the tree outside the school and leave them there for a whole hour; that he would repeatedly pick them up off the ground by their ears or their hair and throw them; and that he would rub an ear hard with a pebble using his finger; along with other methods of torture, some of which he actually would use and some of which were the inventions of the children's imaginations.

Because our boy knew nothing of the four marvelous exercises, and nothing of *saghadun* or *soladun* or *marsh*, he felt absolutely certain that he would suffer these unbearable tortures. Also, because the particular way in which he had been raised did not include beatings as a means of discipline and because he had been somewhat pampered and spoiled at home, he could hardly imagine that he could bear any such suffering. Therefore, it was safer and better to flee from this hell.

So no sooner had the bell ending the second class rung—and before the four exercises began—than he had left the school and headed for home, fleeing from what he expected if he chose to stay.

But he did not know the way to his house, for the school was at the far end of town and his house was in the middle of town. He was a child only a little over six years old and had not been allowed to play in the streets and wander through the alleys like the other children, so as to keep his clothes clean and protect him from the filthy morals and foul language of the children of the town. So he had hardly left the school and walked a few steps when he came to one of the many turns in the road to his house and realized that he was lost and that he could not find his way home without help. The sensible solution would have been to go back to the school, because it was still nearby and his father would come, as he had said, for the ten o'clock recess. But this was more than his little nerves could stand and so he fell back on the usual child's recourse and began to cry loudly.

One of the men of that district came up and asked him his name, and when he learned whose son he was he patted him on the back and brought him to a place near his house and left him there after making sure that he now knew his way home. When our little friend realized he was safe from the hell he feared and his nerves calmed down, he realized how much disgrace there was in what he had done—young as he was he could feel this disgrace—and he could not face his family—not out of fear, for he knew he would not be beaten—but out of shame at his unworthy action. He preferred to avoid them and hide himself in the straw shed, which was attached to the house but had a separate door. He closed the door and climbed up onto the straw and fell asleep.

His father was stunned—when he came with his pastry and sweets—to learn that his son had run away from the school, and he returned home angry and embarrassed. When he got home no one yet knew where the child was, so the whole family was sick with worry, and his father went out to look for him in the streets of the town and sent others to scour all the streets leading to the school and to ask of him from all they chanced to meet. Finally one of them met the man who had brought him home, and the man told him what he had done and that reassured them somewhat.

While they were looking for him outside, his mother's heart led her to his hiding place, and she found him there sleeping. She embraced him and lifted him to her shoulder with great compassion. As for him, he woke up but he could not look at her. He buried his face in her breast and began to sob and cry. In vain she tried to get him to tell her why he had fled from school, nor would he tell anyone else in the family. He was too embarrassed to admit to them that he was afraid of the gym master.

3   The Sacred School

A month or so had passed since he had fled school in fear of the gym master. His mother constantly worried and fretted because he did not join in with the other students as she had hoped. She had great ambitions for him that depended entirely on his success at the primary school, after which he would travel to Cairo, where he would stay at his uncle's and complete his education, thereby realizing the great hopes she had placed in her small child. His older brother (he was actually only his half-brother) constantly taunted him for having run away from school. The child resented this taunting and so dared to do something that he had never done before or since, something his family training totally rejected. He threw the cover of a jar at him and ran. On the other hand, his father did not direct a single word to him, and this was worse than his brother's taunts.

In the end, he found that he had to return to school, but this time without fuss and ceremony or any particular preparation. One morning he simply found himself rising and putting on his uniform. He then made his way to the house of his aunt and called her son and told him he was going to school with him that day.

He was welcomed there by the *'arif* and by the *faqih* (who was called the headmaster) and asked the reason for his absence. Now he realized that his secret had been weighing on him, and he unburdened himself to the teacher, telling him that he was afraid of the

15

gym master. The headmaster was a wise man who proceeded to reassure him on this score until he really felt confident. And so the child realized that he was safe from the danger of this sick devil. He would learn the physical exercises and procedures and, because he was yet small, would be given a long period in which to perfect them. Then—and this is most important—the headmaster would make sure that the gym master would treat him well when he came.

The incubus was lifted from his chest. Upon his return home in the afternoon, they all ceased to worry about him. When he informed his mother about what had happened, she rejoiced in all her being and drew him to her breast in a torrent of emotion. She awaited the arrival of his father to inform him of the happy news. Upon hearing it, his father smiled inside, although outwardly he pretended not to make much of it. He replied to her jokingly: "Spare us, oh, woman, you and your son!"

The school was made up of three interconnected rooms. Along the whole front of it was the schoolyard with the exit gate. There were five grades of students distributed in the rooms in the following manner: The fourth grade, containing the older students, including those aged twenty or more, along with the third grade, whose students were a little younger, were instructed by the headmaster of the school. The other teacher taught the first and second grades in a second room. The kindergarten met in a separate room. And who looked after their education but Ibrahim, the school janitor. Yes! He would finish his job sweeping the school and then fill the pitcher from which the students drank, drawing the water from two big clay pots located within a wooden closet. He would wipe off the slates and distribute chalk to the classrooms and then switch to a teaching role to take care of the young ones in the kindergarten! This alone was enough to put the child off from staying in the kindergarten. What is more, his cousin was in the fourth year. He expressed his desire to relocate to the headmaster, and after negotiations involving the 'arif it was agreed that the child should be in one of the grades—first or second—that the 'arif taught, though in fact he sometimes went to the fourth-year room to sit beside his cousin. Whenever the inspector came to the school, however, he had to return to the kindergarten and remain there until the inspector had left.

The 'arif and the headmaster treated him very well. This was hardly surprising, for every morning the child would bring for them quantities of sugar and tea, which he carried in his pockets. They would entrust these to Ibrahim, who would use them to prepare refreshments during recess and after lunch. Furthermore, his father visited regularly. For all these reasons, the teachers gave him individual attention in class. They wrote the letters of the alphabet, then words, and then sentences on the slate board and left him to copy them. Each day he made progress. In common with a very small number of other students from the village's wealthy families, he received what virtually amounted to special lessons. At the end of the year he was qualified to move on and take a seat in the first year, where he now belonged. He was now accustomed to the school environment and had begun to be a real student.

The school took a step forward the following year. A second teacher was appointed. Ibrahim, consequently, was released from his teaching duties, although he continued with his janitorial work. The schedules were changed: The two teachers and the headmaster now alternated among the three classrooms composed of the five grades. Furthermore, the kindergarten was placed in the same room as the first grade, while the second and third grades were placed in another room. The fourth grade was in a room by itself, where also was found the principal's cabinet, which contained the students' supplies, including erasers, pens, books, and notepads.

But in the year that followed—when the child had passed into the second grade—a big disturbance convulsed the village. The provincial council now had a large number of *fuqaha* trained as teachers and so it seemed obvious that they should put one of them in place of the *shaykh* who was a Qur'an reciter and *kuttab* master but did not have a teaching certificate and knew nothing of arithmetic or any other modern subject. When this step was taken, rumors flooded through the village and shook it to its core. "The government wants to obliterate the Qur'an by neglecting its memorization in the schools!" Was there any better proof of this than the removal of Shaykh Ahmad, who recited the Qur'an and whose presence gave them the confidence to send their children there? The rumors spread like wildfire. Naturally, the *shaykh* fanned the flames in an attempt to gain revenge against the school and to promote the *kuttab*, where he would return to teach. The school lost a very large number of its students, who left it to follow "Our Master" Shaykh Ahmad in order to gain his *baraka*, the *baraka* of his *kuttab* and the *baraka* of God's Word, thereby protecting their religion from the school of unbelief and error by which the government would steal their religion from them without their realizing it.

"Our Master" did not fail to call on the child's father to notify him of the momentous news and to warn him against keeping his son in the school, and he stated his strong hope that the boy would go to the *kuttab* the very next day. His father was too sensible to be taken in by this claim. He read the press and subscribed to the daily newspaper. And he was a member of the village committee of the Nationalist Party.[1] But he was timid and polite and did not want to hurt the feelings of Our Master—the son of his own master—and so promised him that the child would attend the *kuttab* the next morning.

This turnabout caused a storm in the house. His mother insisted that he remain in the school, for it was the key to the great hopes that she had pinned on the small child. But his father had given his word, and a man never goes back on his word!

Inevitably, his father's view carried the day and the child made his way the next morning to the *kuttab*. He does not remember his small heart ever feeling as much anxiety as it did on that day, or his breast being so constricted and narrowed. Our Master, Shaykh Ahmad, received him kindly with smiles and promptly sat him down beside himself, whereas the other youths of the *kuttab* sat on a mat in the middle of the room or on a bench running around the wall of the room. But none of this decreased his resistance. He was accustomed to being greeted each morning by that neat clean building, with its rooms whitewashed and its courtyard spread with sand. He was used to sitting in the school chairs with their receptacles for books, implements, notepads, and his fine writing slate. In the *kuttab*, by contrast, there were no seats with book receptacles, nor bells, classrooms, books, inkwells, chairs. Instead there was a tin sheet upon which the students would write with ink made from indigo or lamp soot or a similar substance. The students carried their inkwells and pens in their hands wherever they went. If they recited what was on their slates to Our Master and he found that they had memorized it, then they would clean them and write other verses of the Qur'an on them. Their manner of erasing them was filthy, because they would spit on them, rub them with their hands, and then wipe them off with the edge of their garments. Consequently their clothes were always stained with ink.

He was appalled by the fact that Our Master, when he was correcting the slates with red ink and noticed an error in what was written, would promptly lick off the incorrect words with his tongue and then wipe the slate clean with the edge of his palm. The student would then write the correct words. If a student needed to go out to attend a call of nature he did not raise his finger, as did the students in the school; rather he snapped his fingers and called out: "Our Master! Our Master!" If Our Master acknowledged the request he would touch together the fingers of his two hands and say: "Permission granted!" Then the student would leave and might possibly not return for the rest of the day.

In any case, our child's soul was filled with repugnance at everything that surrounded him. He felt bitter, abject loneliness. When he returned to his house he was determined that he would never go back to that filthy place, no matter how much he might be threatened or reproached. He confided this urgent desire to his mother, and her eyes filled with tears.

In the morning his father and Our Master believed that he was going to the *kuttab*. But instead he went to the school by a hidden route, walking very fast, as if he were afraid that someone might follow him. He arrived very early and did not find anyone there, not even the janitor. The door was still locked and so he chose to sit with his back against the door as though he was seeking shelter at a place beloved and protective. After a while the students began to gather, some of whom asked him why he had been absent the day before, because it was the only day he had missed since coming to school. He proceeded to explain to them how he had gone to the *kuttab*, and how he had found it to be unbearably filthy and different in every respect from the beautiful school. All of a sudden he was transformed into a propagandist for the school against the *kuttab*, even though he did not know what propaganda was. When the headmaster asked him for the reason for his unusual absence, he proceeded to tell him the circumstances of the tragedy while the tears streamed from his eyes. The headmaster calmed him down and reassured him that he still had a place at the school and promised to go that very day to his father and convince him that he should remain there.

He did calm down and found himself breathing easily in his familiar environment. When it came time to leave he went to the headmaster and reminded him of his promise, and the headmaster said that he would come right away. And so he did. He arrived at the house with his two colleagues and they convinced the father that his son would be wasted in the *kuttab*. They said that he was an intelligent and outstanding student and that they anticipated a good future for him at the school. Seeing that they were not from the village but were guests, his father felt compelled to accept their wishes. This was his excuse to Our Master when he came again. And so Our Master turned away from him, saying, "There is no power and no strength save in God" and took refuge from the apostles of unbelief and error.

From the day he returned, the school became for him a holy place, like a *mihrab*[2] for prayer. Everything and everyone associated with it rose several degrees in his eyes. He went out of his way to become the school's missionary in its struggle against the *kuttab*.

The main argument for the *kuttab* was that its students memorized the Qur'an, while the school neglected this and was not in fact able to graduate one student who had memorized it. And so he applied himself to memorizing the Qur'an so that he might destroy this main argument. He put a great strain on himself and his health, staying awake until midnight each night going over everything that he had previously memorized. And that was on top of his other studies. By the time the year had ended he had memorized one-third of the Qur'an excellently and would compete in recitation with anyone who challenged him. Then he formed a team of students from the school against the "*kuttab* boys," a team to compete in everything, including memorizing the Qur'an. Therefore, some of the students were selected to memorize particular verses and *suwar* from the Qur'an to be tested on them for the sake of the competition between the two groups. Often the school emerged victorious. These victories made him feel overwhelmingly elated.

The school team took pride in many things. Their neat and tidy building stood in contrast to the old, dirty *kuttab*. The school had a spacious yard and two shady trees with beautiful flowers that could not be found anywhere else in the village. The flowers were "Pasha's Beard" that gave off a fragrant smell. There was the *mazyarah*, a wooden closet with two large water jugs on iron stands nestled within it. Two clean buckets were situated under the water containers to collect the filtered drinking water for the *effendis*,[3] who consisted of the teachers and the school's headmaster—here *shaykhs* counted as *effendis*. The students and other villagers called them *effendis* to distinguish them from the *shaykhs* of the village, whose mark of distinction was that they had memorized the Qur'an. The *effendis* had clean clothes and their salaries were drawn from the provincial council, rather than from the children's weekly tithe that came each Thursday. There were also the chairs and book receptacles and especially the implements that were supplied to them each year, including four notebooks and four manufactured pens. The boys at the *kuttab*, in contrast, wrote on a tin slate with ordinary reed pens. The students at the school received blotting paper to dry their notebooks. In contrast, the boys at the *kuttab* used dirt to dry their slates. They spit on them and rubbed them with their sleeve, or sometimes licked them with their tongues.

There were many other things that made them proud. But nothing compared to the sign that was mounted on top of the gate of the school. This was something unique to the school, and there was nothing like it in the entire village. It had been brought from the provincial capital.[4] The story of this sign actually relates to the following year, by which time the boy had passed into the third grade. The council had an abundance of graduates of the teaching schools that were part of its new system, two of which were then appointed to the school. One of them replaced the old headmaster, who transferred to another village, while the other came as a teacher. At that time there was only one *'arif* left at the school, and he also was transferred a month later. As a result, the school was raised up to another level, as it now met all of the requirements of a government school.

The older students, or, more precisely, those who were now men with moustaches, were weeded out and the kindergarten was abolished. The school was divided into four properly ordered sections.

The new headmaster decided to implement a major change, proposing to put up a sign with the name of the school, just like the schools of the provincial capital. After announcing that the sign was going to cost twenty-five piastres,[5] he suggested that the students should contribute anything they could. The plan excited our boy, for the sign would be another point of pride for the school in its competition with the students of the *kuttab*. And so when some of the students began to bring one or two milliemes, and the sons of the wealthy were donating half a piastre or, in rare cases, an entire piastre, he was doing his best at home to bring in fifty milliemes.

When the sign was finally completed in the provincial capital and then hung over the gate of the school, he was overcome with happiness.

By the end of his fourth year he was doing well in his memorization of the Qur'an, and this was a great miracle for the school, which silenced the tongues and deceitful propaganda of the supporters and youth of the *katatib*. He completed his studies at the school when he was still a child of about ten years. But he had companions who had first completed the memorization of the Qur'an at the *kuttab* and then had entered the school. As a result, they were over fifteen years of age by the time they entered the fourth year. Three of these were able at the end of that year to proceed to the primary teachers' college in the provincial capital. This was a new event in the village, and it had a profound impact upon him. In a few years these three would become *effendis*, like the *effendis* of the school under whom they had studied.

He wished he could blink his eyes and find that he was the same age as they and thus was accepted into the teachers' school. But what right did he have to such dreams? He harbored for these *effendis* a feeling that almost amounted to worship. In the first place, they were part of the "sacred school." In the second place, they knew things that he didn't know and they could do everything. They had a special kind of life whose true nature he could no more understand than he could that of ghosts or spirits.

Today, more than twenty-five years later when circumstances and conditions have changed, he recalls the time he was sent to their home in the village. This house had been donated by one of its owners for them to live in, in recognition of their merit. He recalls that one of them had forgotten his watch and had given him the key so that he could fetch it, for he was known at school for his honesty. He remembers that he entered the house respectfully and with apprehension. It was as though he were entering a holy *mihrab* or an enchanted place. He held his breath as he went up the steps, opened the door into the holy room, and grabbed the watch. He then locked the door and returned as though he were a "clever Hasan" [6] who had come across an enchanted treasure. He wanted to enter the school to which they had been admitted, but his age stood in the way. Inevitably, he had to leave his own school and make a place for a newcomer.

How hard it was for him to leave this small "homeland" and to distance himself from his companions and schoolmates whom he loved and who loved him. And how difficult it was for the teachers at the school to give him up, for he was their first proof that the school could succeed at Qur'an memorization. So they found a way around the problem by registering his name in the fourth-year class as a newcomer a month after the start of the following year. In this manner he returned to his beloved school to spend another year between its walls, in addition to the other happy and beautiful years.

A quarter-century has passed, during which he traveled to Cairo, finished his higher studies, and worked in various positions. But today if he returns to the village he always heads for the holy school, and when he crosses the threshold he feels again the awe he felt in his school days and a humble reverence, and if he were asked his sweetest wishes, he would say that he wished he could again be a student in the sacred school, defending it from the *kuttab* and the *kuttab* boys. When he steps across the sacred threshold, dozens of marvelous and beloved pictures leap through his imagination and dance in his mind as if he were living them again.

He recalls those periods when the school used to be converted into a peninsula surrounded by water on three sides, with only the fourth side remaining as a way of access. This occurred during the time of Nile flood, when the land of the village was covered by water for two months every year in preparation for the year's agriculture. Because the school was located at the edge of the village beside the fields, the waters of the flood surrounded it during these two beautiful months, except for one path in.

The beauty of these two months was especially evident on Saturdays. The *effendis*, some of whom were from the provincial capital and some from the neighboring villages, would stay in the village during the week, go to see their families on Thursdays and Fridays, and then return on Saturday morning. For most of the year they would mount their donkeys at the appropriate time and arrive just before the school bell rang on Saturday morning. During the time of the flood, however, they would take skiffs and sailboats. These did not keep to any schedule and usually did not arrive until almost ten o'clock, so that they would miss the first two classes. And on some beautiful Saturdays they might not arrive until noon!

On such occasions the students used to stand on the shore or go farther into the nearby streets of the village, or else jump and shout in

the courtyard of the school. They would run in and out of the rooms
without any hesitancy or restriction. They had a great time coming
and going and climbing on top of the chairs and book receptacles and
spying from the windows, which faced the floodwaters. Some were
so daring as to take off their clothes and throw themselves into the
water from the windows. They would swim and climb back in
through the windows, where they found their clothes, although
sometimes their companions took the opportunity to hide their
clothes or take them away, forcing them to search about the school
for them, naked, until they finally found them.

These humorous pranks would continue until a sailboat or skiff
approached from across the floodwaters. They would fear that one of
the *effendis* might be in this boat (each would each arrive in a different
boat from their various locales). In the blink of an eye everyone
would be in his chair, with either a Qur'an or a book in front of him.
Order was reestablished and voices fell silent, except for the murmur
of reading, which proved the strength of their concentration.

And so if one of the teachers were in the boat, it was all right. All
of the students were in perfect order. But if the boat were empty,
everything would start up again and the commotion would be even
greater than before. They would return to jumping and leaping into
the water from the windows and on to the ground of the courtyard.
This was repeated every Saturday during the time of the flood. All of
this took place in spite of the efforts of Our Master Abdullah.

Our Master Abdullah was the successor of Ibrahim, the janitor.
He was one of the inhabitants of the village and had been appointed
janitor of the school. Previously he had been an *'arif* in the *kuttab*. He
was pleased to be at the school because the fixed salary of ninety piastres per month was better than the tithes that he had received from
the students at the *kuttab*, which might not exceed five piastres per
month. Although he now worked as a servant, he kept his old title,
"Our Master" Abdullah.

The boy also remembers an incident involving one of the school inspectors. Although it was horrible at the time it now appears delightfully humorous. Two elderly inspectors used to visit the school: one of them was from the provincial council, the other from the Ministry of Education. The presence of either one of them was enough to dry the saliva in the throats of the children and instill fear in their hearts, not to mention turning the teachers and the school upside down, and casting a dark shadow and a suffocating atmosphere over everything. Of the two, the inspector from the ministry inspired the most fear.

He was a tall man with a dark complexion, harsh features, and piercing eyes. He seemed always to be angry at something, snarling and full of rage. As an inspector of the ministry, he inevitably assumed that his visit was of more importance than the visit of the other inspector. Therefore he would appear graver and more violent and rougher in his movements, words, and expressions than was necessary. The *jubba* and *quftan* that covered his tall body made him all the more awesome and terrifying. The teachers were terrified of him and their fear infected the students, so that the hours he spent at school seemed to be an eternity, and time slowed to a crawl.

As for the unforgettable event, it was as follows. Studies were progressing in a leisurely way, as usual. At the end of the year the weather was scorching hot and the students were lazy. The teacher's *jubba* burdened him, so he took it off and threw it over the back of the chair. His turban felt hot and heavy so he took it gently by the tassel so that it would not be mussed and flung it onto the book receptacle of his first student. He then sat on his chair in a relaxed position that allowed his *quftan* to open, the waistband dangling carelessly.

Meanwhile time passed by and the world was quiet. Everyone was dozing sweetly. All of a sudden, a tall and lofty figure jumped through the window and dropped into the classroom, and was among them in an instant. The students were frightened. The blood froze in their veins as they stared at this sudden apparition. They began to scream in fear. The teacher scrambled to his feet, grabbing his turban with one hand and trying unsuccessfully to put on his *jubba* with the other. The apparition opened his lips to display a grim smile. While he shook his head, his tongue uttered sarcastically: "*Mashallah, mashallah.*"[7]

What was going on?

It was the inspector. The inspector from the ministry had as usual been riding a donkey to get from the provincial capital to the village and had stopped under the window to listen. Then he had stood on the back of the donkey in order to reach up to the window to climb in, catching everyone by surprise. This was a novel way of inspecting!

There is another image that he is unable to forget:

The schools and their students experienced a continuing succession of headmasters and teachers on account of the usual yearly transfers. When he was in the fourth year an old *shaykh*, who had received his education at the Azhar and then had joined the provincial council, was appointed headmaster. The man was gray and balding except for a circle of hair that was completely revealed whenever he removed his turban. His baldness made him the laughing stock of the devilish students and the butt of their ridicule. One day these demons conspired against him. As he sat engrossed in correcting notebooks with the students gathered around him, they saw his turban rise gradually from his head and travel to the middle of the room. Then, suddenly, it dropped when the *shaykh* got up and roared in anger, while the students broke out laughing. Tears came to their eyes as they tried to stifle their guffaws. The game of fishhook and line had done its job on the poor *shaykh*'s turban! Just as he had noticed the prank, the student had dropped the line and the turban suddenly fell.

This *shaykh* was infatuated with grammatical endings.[8] The students were young and in primary school, but the *shaykh* did not care. He would call a student to write on the blackboard because his own handwriting was illegible, and would dictate verses of poetry to him and assign the students the task of putting on the endings. If they did not know them, well, bless him, he would make them memorize the endings! It did not matter to the *shaykh* that the students did not understand anything about the profound technicalities of Arabic case endings. It was not unusual to hear a small student stammering out words such as the following: "*Watani* [my homeland] is the subject of a sentence and has a nominative ending that is understood but does not appear because its space is occupied by the first person possessive suffix," or "*Idha* [if, when] is an adverb introducing future action which puts its protasis in the genitive and is itself accusative by virtue of its apodosis."

In any case, the memories of the students were crowded with many such things. Days passed. Scholars and students of the Azhar would come to the village during the holidays. One of these scholars volunteered to give a lesson in the interpretation of the Qur'an to the people in one of the mosques of the village. This lesson consisted simply of the *shaykh* sitting with the illiterate villagers gathered around him and pulling out from his robes a fascicle of al-Zamakhshari's commentary on the Qur'an,[9] which he proceeded to read to them. He would clap his hands from time to time, saying: "Understood?" Some replied, "Understood." Then he continued pouring into their ears everything in Zamakhshari that dealt with grammar, rhetoric, and interpretation, of which they knew nothing.

The boy attended these lessons so that he might become a man. One night the *shaykh* read the interpretation of the Sura of the Cave and recited the following: "This is what we sought for (*nabghi*). So they returned retracing their footsteps." The boy was eager to show off the grammar that he had learned and had noticed that the word *nabghi* was shortened without evident justification. He raised his finger as he would at school and said: "Oh master *shaykh*, why did you shorten the word *nabghi* without a reason?" The *shaykh* raised his head without concern and proceeded to say as though he were still reading: "Sir, the 'ya' was deleted by discretion for ease of pronunciation." He continued on without further ado and paid no more attention to the small boy.

The boy heard "by discretion for ease of pronunciation" and found that this was not in his field of understanding. He knew the ending for the conditional and the ending for the vocative. And he knew the deleted letters and the weak letters, but he was not capable of understanding the words "by discretion for ease of pronunciation." Truly it was the knowledge of the Azhar, and here he was in the village. However much you know, someone knows more. Many years passed before the boy could understand "by discretion" and "for ease of pronunciation."

He recalls other things that made a greater impression upon him. The school finally opened its doors to the girls in the village, so that they could study with the boys throughout the day, because the system of dividing the school day between boys and girls had not yet been devised for the villages. Some of the fathers agreed to send their daughters to the school—especially if they were small children not above the age of ten. There were only seven such girls in the entire school. Although they were no different from the other girls in the village, their presence at the school produced a strange atmosphere and diffused a particular aroma. This atmosphere was a mixture, on one hand, of sharp sensitivity and a hidden desire to speak with this

strange sex in the school, and on the other hand, a naïve rustic timid-
ity and a fear of punishment both at school and at home for overstep-
ping the bounds.

But all of this did not prevent some of the boys, especially the
older ones, from teasing the girls with words, some of which were
distasteful as they were leaving the school, and with playful gestures
and sounds. Of course, the purpose of these was to attract attention.
In his case, his extreme shyness and his family training kept him far
away from this kind of behavior. But this did not mean that he had
less desire than others to attract attention. His way of accomplishing
this was compatible with his upbringing. He put himself forward as
the defender of the girls' honor when they were attacked.

Moreover, he was surprised to win the battle without a struggle.
One day he was at home when all of a sudden there were seven girls
knocking at the door, asking to play with his little sister in the house.
The fact that one of the girls was the sister of the wife of one of his
uncles made this more socially acceptable. Also among them was her
cousin and for this cousin he had a special feeling. With the former he
was permitted to converse freely. With the latter, even though the
fact of their distant relationship allowed them to converse, he was
scared to death to talk to her and would avoid it with Sufi-like piety
and out of a deep sense of shyness. In any case, he did not invite them
to enter the house, nor was he even capable of doing so. But when
they all arrived together in such a way, led by the first little girl, with
the other acting enticingly shy, he felt in himself an elation that he
had never felt before. He recognized that they were really interested
in him, not his little sister. He sensed that the other girl felt that he
was special, just as he felt she was, even though they did not exchange a word. These visits were repeated, though they were no
more than brief encounters. Still, they left a trace in him that could
not be erased.

This other girl was bronze-skinned and her face showed a special, indeed unique, character. By village standards she was not beautiful. She did not have a white complexion, her nose was not defined to the right proportions, and her mouth did not resemble the "Signet-ring of Solomon." But she alone among the girls of the school, indeed of the whole village, looked beautiful in his eyes. For him, the secret of her beauty lay in her special character, even though at that time he did not understand that "special character." When he left the village for Cairo, this face remained in his imagination and defined the ideal of beauty for him. So when he returned three years later, his life, culture, and worldview having changed, the first question he asked, cautiously and indirectly, was about the fate of that girl who had been his first infatuation. He learned that she was married and lived far from the village. He had to excuse himself from the group because he felt his eyes filling with tears.

4   Medical Mission

It was almost ten o'clock in the morning. They had already had the first and second periods in the village school. Then they were turned loose and burst forth from the classes like birds released from a cage after a long confinement. They burst forth running and jumping, screaming and shouting at each other, for no other reason than to confirm to themselves that they were free after the long confinement. Then they proceeded to transfer the snacks they carried from their pockets to their stomachs. They had been carrying them for two hours but the classroom "order" would not allow them to dig into their pockets there. Then those from the richer families would go off to Uncle Khalil's shack and buy a millieme's worth of dates and sugar-cane from him.

And this was not the only value of the "recess," for the children had other needs during that short space of fifteen minutes. The school was at the edge of the village, bordering on a large field, and if the function of the field was to grow food and fodder for men and beasts, it also had another function for the schoolchildren and other villagers. It served as a public toilet. The children burst forth in every direction, emptying the contents of their pockets into their stomachs and the contents of their stomachs into the neighboring field. But suddenly the bell rang violently and continuously before the proper time for the third period, and although they of course did not wear watches, they knew without fail the exact time, for their instinct very rarely failed them.

They lined up in rows, but they did not hear the accustomed calls to which they performed the simple exercises, *saghadun*, or "right face," *suladun*, or "left face," or *marsh*, or "go to class." It was not this they heard but the school principal giving them the strange and marvelous news that they were about to go to the *'umda*'s residence and that they would march there in strict order.[1] This meant that they would have to pass through almost all of the streets of the village because the *'umda*'s residence was at the far end of town. The headmaster warned them against getting out of line as they marched or looking either to the right or the left, especially when they passed the village's small market where sugarcane, dates, and the sour local apples were on display.

They were going to the *'umda*'s residence? Why? They had never entered this house before, although their parents and relatives had told them that they had gone there on occasion when one of the watchmen had summoned them to pay back taxes or the watchmens' fees or to give witness or because of complaints from some of the *fellahin*. As for them, they were schoolchildren. What did they have to do with all these things?

Our child was a bit bold with the headmaster and the teachers, because he was outstanding in his lessons and, more importantly, was the son of a man known for hospitality with some claim to enlightenment, who mixed with the *effendis* and often received them at home, and this was no small thing.

As I say, he was bold with the *effendis* and so dared to ask, "Why are we going to the *'umda*'s residence?"

He asked—and wished he hadn't asked! The answer bespoke a greater calamity than either he or his companions had imagined. The physician, that is, the medical doctor, was there and demanded to see them all.

The doctor? Oh, horrors! Surely today was the end for all of them. For in their experience the doctor only came to the village on a grim day when someone had been killed. Then he would come accompanying the legal officer to dissect the body.

The legal officer and the doctor—these were the two most terrifying and fearsome beings in the whole village. In the minds of the children they were vague and unformed things, without shape or size, so that their little imaginations could picture them as they chose, and not necessarily as ordinary people or things. To be sure, there were also other people whom they feared, such as the reconnaissance patrol, a group of soldiers who would visit the village at night to see whether the watchmen were awake and doing their duty and to arrest anyone they found out on the village streets or the roads leading into it after midnight. There were also the adjutant (*mu'awin*), the superintendent (*mulahiz*), and the district commissioner (*ma'mur*), who rarely visited the village unless accompanying the legal officer and the doctor, but they were not as fearful as the legal officer and the doctor in the imagination of the village as a whole, and particularly in the imaginations of the children.

And now here was the doctor demanding to see them, demanding them specifically. What was going on? They had absolutely no idea why he wanted to see them. But from the bottom of their hearts they knew that it could be nothing good, and that they certainly would not leave the *'umda*'s residence as safe and sound as when they went in.

And what was the doctor's job? Wasn't it to cut up the corpses of dead people? Wasn't it to split open the bellies of the injured or to cut off their hands and legs simply in order to make them suffer or to examine them for the pleasure of doing so? Or wasn't it to make some sick people drink the "cup," that is, poison, to kill them, so that he would not have to bother treating them or to satisfy the wish of the *'umda*, who would bribe him to get rid of his enemies who were injured in incidents?

What did they have to do with this doctor? They were not dead bodies to be cut up, nor injured people who should have their limbs cut off or be administered the "cup." But surely he would not call for them without some reason. The least would be to administer to them the "surgery," which was the term they used for a vaccination, that fearful operation that was delegated to some of the health assistants and nurses from time to time, alarming the village. Hardly would they announce that the "little doctor" (distinguishing him from the "big doctor," who was now calling for them and who always accompanied the legal officer and never came alone) was in the village . . . hardly would they announce this in the village, than everyone would shake and tremble and mothers would go out into the streets wailing and terrified, gathering their children from everywhere in fear and haste, and then shut themselves in their houses and go up to the roofs, ready to leap from one roof to another. Often these devils would knock at the doors and then break them down with the help of the watchmen and force the "surgery" on whoever was inside. Whoever managed to jump over to the next house would not fail to find the path to safety. Whoever could not would hide in the crop silo or the chicken coop where the doctor would not think to look.

This was the doctor they knew. What could they think about the big doctor who came only with the legal officer? Surely no one who fell into his hands could escape except by a miracle of fate or by the *baraka* of an amulet from one of the great *awliya*. All their bones shook when they heard the distressing news; their faces turned pale and some of them loudly wept and wailed. Vainly did the *effendis* try to calm their terrors and restore their confidence by assuring them that they would accompany them and would not leave them alone.

Would accompany them! What did that mean? It was the doctor they were going to, so what was this song and dance from the *effendis* and their ilk? With all their great respect for them and even their belief that the *effendis* were made of different clay from that of the ordinary villagers, still, the situation today involved the doctor, not some human matter in which human beings might be of help.

Fate had to have its way. They had been told that it was no use trying to run away, and that they would be led in line guarded by the town watchmen and supervised by the *effendis,* and that their names had already been given to the doctor from the school rolls, so if anyone ran away he would be caught and punished! So there was no escape from what was fated. What would be, would be! But couldn't they tell their folks and see their homes and families before being herded off to their unknown fate? This too was forbidden, they were told. So they marched off with their heads hanging.

God only knows how they arrived at the *'umda*'s house, but arrive they did! They stood in a long line, whose front was inside the reception room—that is, in the danger zone—and whose end was out in the street. On the right and the left stood the watchmen with their guns and their tall felt headgear, while one of the *effendis* stood at the head of the line and one at the end. As for the director, he went ahead of them to the doctor, so as to give them a bit of confidence and to provide the appearance of the courage demanded.

The line was arranged so that the older students went first and the younger or shorter followed them. Only at this moment did shortness become the greatest of God's blessings. As for those who went first, only God knew what was happening to them. As for those who were last, theirs was constant trepidation and anxiety, waiting to see what would happen to those who had gone in first, so as to know what kind of fate awaited them in due time.

Suddenly some of the older ones began to come out while the rest of the younger ones were still in the long line, and there was an outburst of shouts and questions that the watchmen and the *effendis* could not restrain.

"Did you go into the doctor?"

"Yes, we did."

"What did he do to you?"

"Nothing! He pricked our finger with a pin and drew some blood."

Blood! But the sight of them alive and well was reassuring in any case.

"And what is that thing in your hands?"

"A small tin box in which we must put a specimen of feces and a small bottle for a specimen of urine."

"A specimen of feces and a specimen of urine? What for?"

"We don't know. That is what the doctor told us to do."

"The doctor himself told you to do this?"

"No. The big doctor pricked us and the small doctors gave us the box and the bottle and told us to provide the specimen for the doctor."

Their fright receded a bit, only to be replaced by astonished and perplexed puzzlement at this strange demand! No one had ever asked them for anything like this before. What would the doctor do with these extraordinary samples? While they could understand someone pricking them with a pin and drawing blood, they could not understand someone asking for specimens. Pricking and blood were naturally associated with a doctor. But this? Who knows except the doctor?

Though the demand was simple and without cost, it turned out to be difficult and costly in many cases. They were all told to go off to the latrines in the village mosques and come back half an hour later with what was demanded.

Not every child was prepared to comply with such a demand in so short a time, especially since they had relieved themselves during the school recess. Had this been before the recess, everything would still be there, especially the one of the two specimens that cannot be produced simply on demand. As for those who still had something left in their bowels, they went off confidently, but as for those who felt that their bowels would not respond, or who tried and failed, their faces turned pale and their hearts raced from fear. They were overwhelmed by perplexity and terror.

What would they do? How could they return to the reception room? Or, how could they be absent at the appointed time? The least they could imagine happening if they returned empty-handed was that the doctor would cut open their bellies to get the required specimen, or that he would insert a long tube into their bodies to get it. The first case meant death or the risk of death; the second meant shame in the presence of their fellows and before the villagers. Who could protect them from such a fate when they were in with the doctor? However brave and tough their families might be, they had no might or power in the face of this most awesome man from the government, as awesome as the legal officer . . . and that was that!

Now was the time for ingenuity! Now the value of cooperation became evident! The students were brothers, so what better time to show the value of this brotherhood than now?

Now those in need besought their brethren to extend them their aid and to fill their small containers for them. There was a big debate as to whether half a container was enough or whether they had to fill it. The majority held that it had to be filled to the top and this fixed itself in the minds of everyone. Here each one's nature appeared in its true colors, something that is best revealed through adversity. Those children of good background and noble nature came to the aid of their comrades with no hesitation, while as for those of weak background and ignoble nature, some refused to help because of old grudges and others held back out of meanness and selfishness.

But this cooperation only partly fulfilled the need and there remained a large number who could not get what they lacked. Here a genius among them hit upon a brilliant idea. The mosque latrines had an ample supply for all!

To explain how this was, it is necessary to say something about these latrines. There were about ten mosques in the village, all of them constructed in the old manner. Their water systems were extraordinary, for they were composed of a "tank" consisting of a basin made of bricks and coated with cement inside and out. It was filled by a special worker who drew water from the mosque well in a bucket and poured it in till it was full. On the outside wall of the tank, faucets were installed connecting directly to the water inside it and from this the worshippers made their ablutions.

But the tank did not serve only for ablutions. It was also used as a bath by a large number of people who did not have water at home to wash with when needed. So they would go here under the cover of darkness shortly before dawn, climb the wall, raise the wooden lid, and then immerse themselves and cleanse their bodies of their filth, which they would leave there for those coming to make their ablutions.

Adjoining this water system were the latrines. Their construction was extraordinary, for they stood in a long row with a partition separating each one. From inside they were all connected to an open channel in which water ran, passing through an opening in the partition walls that was the width of the channel. This channel was filled by water from the well in the same way the tank was. The worshippers and others in the toilets used this "running" water to cleanse their hands of excrement while the water was running through all the stalls.

As for the latrines themselves, their construction was even more extraordinary. Each latrine consisted of two "footrests" upon which someone would squat to relieve himself. Between them was a wide opening that required the one squatting to spread his legs wide so as not to fall into the pit. What fell into this pit would pile up until it was close to the top, for there were a limited number of mosque latrines and an enormous number who frequented them. It was rare for a house to have a latrine and all the men and older boys had recourse to the mosques or the fields. The women and children found ample space on the flat roofs of the houses.

This would continue throughout the year, and an unbearable odor would issue forth from these open latrines. The fecal matter was in full view of the person who sat there to take care of his needs, and the mosquitoes would alight first on this exposed matter and then on the faces of those sitting there. And after these had left the mosquitoes would make their way to the worshippers and the nearby houses, coming and going as they wished.

At a particular time the *sarbatiyyah*, that is, those who clean out drains and sewers, would be contracted from the nearby city to come and clean out the toilets of one or more mosques. They had an extraordinary way of doing this. Special carts were not used as they are in some cities that lack sewage systems. What call would there be for these carts, when there was a natural way adapted to the agricultural environment? Are not channels used in the fields to carry water from one place to another? Then why not likewise use them to carry this matter from the sewage pits to the fields?

This would work! One only had to dig an open channel from the mosque whose latrine pits were to be cleaned to the fields outside the village, running this channel through the middle of the street past the houses and shops. Then a bucket would be hung from a winch. Two workers, located above the pit, would take turns filling the bucket with the contents of the pit and pouring it into the channel. Soon the current would carry everything to the field that was intended to receive this precious natural fertilizer.

Now it might happen that a number of mosques in different parts of the village would require cleaning at the same time. In order to save digging too many channels, they would link them into a network covering the entire village. Nor would the inhabitants of the houses and stores object for a week or two to "enjoying" the extraordinary sight and strong smell. After all, these are the houses of God and no one should feel inconvenienced by the excretions of the worshippers.*

It was the nearness of the required fecal material to the openings of these marvelous toilets that made possible the brilliant idea that grew in the mind of that genius of a student. It was enough to suggest this to the worried brethren to relieve their anxiety, and it was only minutes before all the containers were full and delivered to the doctors with profound confidence. Then the children were given the rest of the day off and returned to their homes, barely able to believe their luck.

Later we learned that the medical mission had come to collect statistics concerning the conditions of anemia, bilharzia, ancylostomiasis, and escarse. But we never found out what results the mission actually recorded in its official and supposedly reliable statistics.

*Author's note: This method has now changed and covered carts are used in some cities.

5   The Local Doctor

He had not yet begun primary school because he was not yet six
years old. One day morning came, the sun began its climb, and the
time moved on past mid-morning, and lo and behold, everyone in the
house was sick, vomiting, and writhing in pain, even though they had
been full of health and vigor the day before—except for him, because
he had been ill for a number of days. They had eaten a dinner of meat,
two kinds of vegetables, rice, and watermelon. As to why there had
been such variety, it was the *khatma*.

The *khatma* was a seasonal custom in their house, repeated four or
five times a year. It involved inviting some "preachers," that is, Qur'an
reciters, to the house to recite, so that they might seek blessing, good
fortune, and mercy for the spirits of the dead. This happened on specific occasions, such as the Day of 'Ashura, the greater and lesser
'Eids, the twenty-seventh of Rajab, mid-Sha'ban, and also through
the whole month of Ramadan.[1] It was called *"khatma"* (completion)
because four or five reciters would recite the complete text of the
Qur'an during this period. They would do some of it in the most ap-
proved manner, that is, they would recite it aloud with proper ca-
dence, and they would mutter part of it under their breath, and which
they did was left to their conscience. Some—and these were the truly
pious—were very scrupulous and recited their whole section within
their hearts either on the day of the *khatma* or after it. Some of them

stammered and muttered and slurred some of the verses, raising their voices from time to time with an individual word or syllable and then returning to their faint muttering. Then they would announce that they had finished their set section, saying, "Almighty God has spoken the truth."

These reciters were invited the night before the *khatma* in preparation for the next morning. When they had performed the dawn prayer they came to the house and sat in the reception room, reciting the Qur'an in a low voice until the sun rose, when they were offered *iftar*, usually rice cooked with milk or wheat bread crumbs in sweetened milk, if it was the season for milk, from autumn to spring. In summer milk was scarce in the house and in the village, because during this period the milk animals had ceased their milk production in preparation for calving in the autumn, except for those that were not impregnated because they had given birth the previous year and so continued giving milk until the next year. In that case the *iftar* was usually honey and cheese, sometimes with wheat bread and at other times with pastries.

Then they continued reciting the Qur'an, sometimes in raised and properly cadenced voices and sometimes in low voices or muttering so that one could hardly make it out, until noon approached and they went out for their prayers. Then they would return to find the inevitable lunch of wheat bread, cheese, and honey and would eat. Then if it were summertime they would take a nap until the mid-afternoon, or if it were wintertime they would rest and drink tea and cinnamon water and other hot drinks. When it was time for the afternoon prayer they went out to the mosque, though some might perform it in the house. Then they would get together and continue their recitation in a loud voice that most of the neighborhood could hear. This continued until about sunset, when they were brought the principal meal, consisting of meat, vegetables, rice, and fresh or cooked fruit. Some of them, a small minority, would eat in a polite and restrained way, while the vast majority would grab the food voraciously and uncouthly.

The boy still remembers that some would divide the large round flat *shamsi* bread, which is twice the size of city bread, into only four parts and dip each quarter into the bowl of food greedily and ravenously so as to get onto it the largest possible portion of the food. Then they would lift it up while the fat was running all over their hands and onto their legs and dripping onto their clothing and then toss the whole mass into a wide open mouth and, chomping, loudly send it into their gullets while their hands were occupied in bringing up the next bite—and so on until they reached the ninth or tenth round of bread in almost no time. They did the same only more so with the meat and the fruit. Their portions of meat were so generous as to amount to a pound for each one.

For this reason the Qur'an reciters were greatly envied in the village and many people devoted themselves to memorizing the Qur'an, for the reciter was assured of his meals most days of the year and much of the time he ate better food than even the wealthiest in the village. In addition to all this he received a wage that might be as much as five piastres for each *khatma*, although the standard rate was half this.

And the *khatma* days were not the only blessed days in the lives of the reciters, for there were the funeral ceremonies, which went on for seven whole nights in the village and at which the Qur'an sometimes was recited in the afternoon, the nighttime, and the morning, and food was brought for the reciters twice a day, including inevitably a meal of meat and vegetables for the evening meal. Then there was the *tal'a*, which followed the seven days, when the family of the deceased would go to the grave and people would go out to offer their condolences. There the Qur'an was recited and the reciters would receive a considerable amount of pastry. Then they would return to the house and recite a *khatma*, which involved the same things as the separate *khatmas* during the various seasons. All of this was done equally by the poor and the rich. In addition to this excellent food throughout the week, the reciter received a generous fee for livening up the funeral for seven nights. Occasionally this sum could reach upwards of half a pound but more commonly it would be twenty-five milliemes.

As for the "evenings of Ramadan," this was a long and blessed season for the reciters. More than twenty houses in the village held these "evenings" and employed between forty and sixty reciters, and these were the lucky ones whose colleagues looked on them with a jealous eye. Each night they got a splendid *suhur,* and in some houses they got food for the breaking of the fast also. When it was the 'Eid they ate the meal and also got their high wage, usually a pound for each "preacher." So it is no surprise that these were people of note in the village. For they had the *baraka* of the Book of God which they carried in their hearts. They were assured of their livelihood, above reproach, and blessed.

It was the night of mid-Sha'ban and there was a large variety of food. They had taken their evening meal after the "preachers" had eaten and the food had been distributed to the poor. Some of the meat and sliced watermelon remained out all night until the morning. When the next morning came, the family gathered and ate some of the meat with bread and cheese, and some also ate some of the watermelon. Our child, however, was not feeling well and so did not touch the meat. He took only a small piece of the watermelon along with a bite of cheese. That was all he wanted. Not an hour passed before they began to complain of stomachaches. First some and then others went and emptied what was in their stomachs, and then they were overcome with pain and dizziness. Throughout the house arose the refrain, "The food is poisoned!"

At this time the family was still small, made up of the two parents, our child, and his two sisters, one three years older than he and the other three years younger. But this small family included a number of servants who were not really servants, as city-dwellers would understand this term. They were poor people, some of whom were distantly related to the family and some of whom lived nearby. These latter, who included men, women, and children, took care of the household chores—apart from preparing the food, which his mother inevitably reserved for herself—at various times during the day and night. In return for this they received a meal, or some fuel that they needed from animal droppings, or some clothing discarded by the family that these poor people could make use of, and also measures of grain in season and quantities of straw and dry cornstalks for fuel. Their relationship to the immediate family was more like that of other family members than servants. The younger among them called the head of the family "my uncle Hājj," because the child's father had made the hajj, while the older ones simply called him "Hājj," without demeaning themselves by saying "my master" as is the practice in the city.

One after another the family members began to show the signs of poisoning and to raise the cry, "The food is smelled," saying "smelled" rather than "poisoned."[2] By this they referred to the belief that poisoning is caused by certain reptiles smelling the food. Usually they had snakes in mind, or sometimes geckos. Any food that is left uncovered, particularly milk and watermelon, is in danger, in their belief, of being smelled by a snake, who licks it and "squirts" onto it, that is, leaves some of its poisonous saliva on it. Then when people eat it the poison runs quickly through their bodies, as had now happened to all of them.

In less than an hour the news had spread throughout the village and people had begun to come to visit them, individually or in groups, including friends and family as well as many others. The house, in spite of its size, was soon full of visitors of both sexes. His father was lying in the reception room, apart from the women's area, and his place was crowded with men of all classes and ages. Our child and his mother and sisters were in the other section of the house and the visiting women there took up every foot of space. The situation looked quite serious. Past experience from similar situations, which had often occurred the village, was not promising. The real cause was either eating food that had spoiled after being left for two or three days or, alternatively, the copper oxide that had accumulated in the copper pots and pans, but it was always ascribed to the "smelling of snakes."

In their case copper oxide poisoning was unlikely, because special preparations had been made for the occasion and all the pots and pans had that very day been coated with tin. Most likely it was the sliced watermelon that had spoiled and caused this poisoning, because watermelon is often affected by just this kind of contamination, although the leftovers of the watermelon and the other food had been eaten by some of the servants and they were not at all affected. This fact gave rise to another supposition—besides the smelling of snakes—that was . . . envy!

This belief was widespread in the village. And they were indeed envied, envied for many things and especially for their standard of living. Nothing stirred up the villagers' envy so much as the signs of someone else's prosperity. It was enough for people to observe the amount of meat that entered the house, the amount of butter consumed there, and the fruit and other things that only a few people could enjoy, for the feelings of envy to be stirred up in the souls of the majority of the villagers, and they could certainly be pardoned for this. So their opinion inclined toward envy as the explanation of this sudden poisoning of the whole family while the servants who ate the same food were not poisoned. Although there were many other possible explanations for this fact, envy was the first one they thought of.

But his father, who was an enlightened man, would have nothing to do with this explanation, so then the discussion turned to the question of treatment and the appropriate antidote to cure the poisoning.

As for our child, if you could have perceived his real feelings on that day you would have seen him in a state of joy and happiness. What with all this excitement in the house, with people of all sorts and classes filling it, with their coming and going, their expressions of concern for the family and especially for him, because he was the only boy in the family, and with the unceasing movement that never quieted down—all of this stirred up his feelings and gladdened his thoughts. If he had not been indisposed beforehand this joy would have been many times greater. It was not every day that such turmoil and confusion took over the house.

Among these relentlessly moving and numerous crowds there was one man who stood out. He was tall, slender, and of light complexion. He was dressed in a clean, white *gallabiyya*, tailor-made in the urban style, not the village style, with a clean, white scarf over it, and wore elegant leather slippers on his feet. This elegant man who stood out from the whole crowd was issuing orders but in a friendly, gentle, and graceful manner, and his orders had to do with quantities of milk being brought, into which he personally dissolved a special substance and then had them taken to the sick people in glasses. He was the one in charge of treating this vast number of sick people. This man was Sayyid al-Hakim.

You must know that this gentleman was one of the medical assistants who had been dismissed from the government hospital in the district capital, and he had chosen, after his dismissal, to open a "clinic" in the village and thus to enjoy the title of "doctor"! Our child remembers this clinic. It occupied two large clean rooms above two shops in the little village market. How often he had entered this room to have the many wounds bandaged that he got from his sharp penknife, which he always kept to cut sugarcane, to scratch marks onto wooden doors and windows, and to cut empty spools of thread into two halves and make them into zi'ninas, a kind of top into whose hole a date stone of the right size was placed. Then it was spun with the fingers and it would spin for a longer or shorter period of time according to the strength of the player, the spinning capacity of the date stone, and the weight of the top.

He would also take his younger sister there. She was a child and had a problem in her ear. It would secrete a substance that attracted flies, and these would die in her ear and constitute a danger. Then he would take her to Sayyid al-Hakim, who would clean out her ear and remove the dead flies with a rubber tube. Such small operations were not the only ones Sayyid al-Hakim undertook to perform. He would find a cure for all kinds of eye problems, stomach troubles, and chest problems, and many of the "operations" were performed in the clinic or in homes. He opened abscesses anywhere in the body and set simple and compound fractures; in dozens of such simple operations his scalpel moved with confidence. The only kinds of operations that he shied away from were the operations that involved opening the belly. That was not because he couldn't do them, God perish the thought, but because of his sensitive heart and deep faith. These brutal operations were the specialty of the "big doctor," the doctor who came with the legal officer to dismember corpses, split open bellies, and mutilate the dead and the injured. But this kind-hearted, meek, gentle, and elegant man avoided these brutal operations; he was content to be simply sweet, gentle, and merciful. Today, the day of the poisoning, he was in his true element, dispensing compassion and medical treatment.

Now, I would like the reader to know that this Sayyid was the friend of the enlightened men of the village only, and they were the only ones who turned to him when they and their children were struck by afflictions. This distinguished them from the others, who would depend on folk remedies and the barber-surgeons of the village. The friends of this Sayyid were the believers in modern medicine. It happened that all of the people who had suffered poisoning were cured, and this increased his fame and raised his prestige, so that many more came to him, even those who were not believers in modern medicine. The Sayyid's fees were not high, never more than one or two piastres including the price of the medicine. How then did he live on such a small income? You must know that the village was generous and hospitable. He lived at his clinic, which was rent-free, and he seldom had to pay for his meals because every day he was the guest of one of his friends from among the enlightened elite of the village, those who believed in modern medicine and not superstitions and quackery.

It was, however, another event that really caused his reputation to take off and raised him to the height of fame. This happened soon after the case of poisoning and shook the village deeply, because it was caused by a number of factors calling for greatest concern. Among the many *awliya* in the village there was a great living *wali* (*awliya* may be living or dead and they are organized into different classes and levels). He was from a family of *awliya*, one that had inherited sainthood from ages past, and the "medicine" he had received was powerful and weighed heavily on him. His position in the ranks of the *awliya* was surpassed only by the four "renowned" ones, Sayyid al-Badawi, Sidi Ibrahim Desuqi, Sidi 'Abd al-Qadir al-Jilani, and *al-Qutb al-Mutawalli*,[3] and, above all of these, the Qutb al-Ghawth, as has been described in the chapter on the *magzub*.[4]

This living *wali*, Shaykh Bakr, was at a higher level than even Shaykh 'Abd al-Fattah, the deceased *shaykh* whom the villagers followed, who provided the town with its unofficial name, the town of Shaykh 'Abd al-Fattah, and who was of longer standing and had a deeper hold on people's hearts. In view of the strength of the "medicine," the *shaykh* kept alternating between a condition of violent "attraction" (*jadhb*) and a state of calm sainthood. Often the former condition would take control of him and he would remain agitated for a number of days, with no one able to approach him unless that person wished to enjoy the sweetness of his stick so as to treat a sore limb by its blows. This would then be followed by a condition of utter silence and total fasting; he would neither eat, nor speak, nor meet with anyone. He would take no food for a long period except one or two dates with a little water in complete and continual silence. Sometimes he was calm and received the many visitors who came to his house from the various neighboring villages. And how blessed was the one who managed to touch the hem of his garment! As for the one who managed to touch or kiss his hand, he would be triumphant in this world and the next!

The *shaykh* hardly spoke any clear words, but rather brief sounds and obscure mumblings. Of course, for every sound there was an interpretation and for every mumbling a meaning. These interpretations were provided by those close to the *shaykh*, members of his family and other close followers. If they were for good, they informed the people involved, and if for bad they alleged that they had no knowledge of the *shaykh*'s purposes, which were known only to God. In the latter case the people perceived that their need would not be met and that they would be disappointed, so let them wait for another moment when the *shaykh* would be more pleased with them and more inclined to respond, or when the gates of heaven would be open and would respond to them by answering the *shaykh*'s prayers, and he would not pray unless he was certain of an answer.

The *shaykh* bathed only rarely, but when he did his leftover bath water, which carried the treasures of his body, was considered to be sacred. His family kept it to distribute in discreet quantities to his waiting followers. Some would drink it, some would bathe their eyes in it, and some would keep it in bottles for times of need. To the house of this *wali* flocked delegations of people and gifts abounded, each reflecting the financial ability of the bearer. The house was the destination of visitors from all directions, some pouring resources into it and others seeking help from it, with tireless movement and blessings galore—all through the *baraka* of the great *shaykh*. And besides all this, the house was . . . a hospital!

Every sick person whose cure proved difficult attached himself closely to the *shaykh*'s house. Such men were not content with intermittent visits and *baraka*. But not all men could enjoy this sojourn. It was for the inner elite of families with longstanding ties of friendship, those who were of consequence in the view of the *shaykh* and his family. Otherwise the rooms and courtyard could not have accommodated all who wished to stay.

Among those blessed by closeness to the *shaykh* was a young lady from a highly placed and wealthy family from a nearby town. She had been stricken with madness and her people had brought her to the *shaykh*'s house. The gates of heaven proved to be open and the *shaykh* responded to them and gave permission for her to reside there. So she was assigned a furnished room in which to stay with her personal servant-woman who had raised her, as was the practice among the daughters of the wealthy in Upper Egypt.

We have no need to describe the presents that were brought to the *shaykh*'s house during such a cherished sojourn, but suffice it to say that two camels laden with farm produce, meat, sweets, sugar, and fruit used to enter the village every week and unloaded these at the *shaykh*'s house, not to mention clothing and money.

One night the people awoke to shrill screaming, wailing, and pleas for help. They roused themselves from their sleep to see fire blazing in the *shaykh*'s house. It was a serious fire and such fires in the village were a threat to all, especially in the summer after the harvest was brought in and the stalks of corn and cotton to be used for fuel were stored on the roofs, because these were the only storage places available to the villagers in their houses. Of no avail were the repeated calls by the government against storing fuel on the roofs because of the danger of fire. As the well-known saying goes, if you want to be obeyed, command what is possible. The villagers did not obey these commands of the government because they were impossible!

It was usual in such a situation that the family would awaken to see the fire blazing in their house, and the women would cry out lamenting and calling to be rescued and the men would raise their voices calling for aid: "Come on, guys, come on!" This was a warning call, to bring people from every direction and to awaken the water carriers in particular, who carried the water skins that they filled with water from the wells with enormous effort, because they had to use pulleys, ropes, and buckets to draw from the bottoms of the deep wells. Then they would carry these water skins on their backs for long distances to fight the fire, which in no time jumped from house to house because the houses were so close together, because their roofs touched, and because inflammable material was near at hand. Either they would close the mouth of the water skin down to a small opening and then squeeze it, so that the water would come out with some degree of force and reach some height, albeit limited, or they would climb onto the neighboring houses and pour the water onto the fire from there if the situation permitted, while the rest of the men would try to save the inhabitants.

Perhaps one of the well-off city dwellers will ask, "Where were the fire engines?" Fire engines? Fire engines are in the city, my dear sir, and it is a vast distance between the city and the village!

The whole village awoke as it usually did for every incident, and became wide awake when rumor had it that the fire was in the *shaykh*'s house. In the *shaykh*'s house? Was that possible? Could the *shaykh*'s house burn when the *shaykh* was in it? Yes, it was possible, but there had to be a reason. And it had to be that the *shaykh* was angry with someone in the house. Presently the name of this person was announced. It was his son, who had caused his older son to move away due to his quarrelling and violence against the will of the *shaykh*. "There is no power and no strength except through God the Almighty." In any case, they rushed to put out the fire with all the strength they could muster. The *shaykh's* anger would inevitably cool and his agitation would calm down, but it was necessary to put out the fire first, because fire is a fearful and terrifying thing.

It became clear after a time that the fire had consumed an entire wing of the house, this being the wing occupied by this son and his wife and also containing the room assigned to the mad girl. When the situation had calmed down and morning had come, and they began to inspect everything, they found the son and his wife safe, because they had escaped before the fire could consume them. When they looked in the girl's room they found a body so badly burned it had turned to charcoal and they found nothing else. People were violently shaken and rudely shocked, but this is what fate had ordained!

There was no way to avoid informing the provincial center of this incident, because a life had been lost and another person, beside the victim, had gone missing and they did not know anything about her fate. Thus the *'umda* could not cover up the incident, as happened in the majority of these cases and others, which involved robbery and quarrelling but did not get to the point of killing.

It was necessary, then, for the legal officer and with him the big doctor to examine the body and determine who had been burned, the mad girl or her servant. One could not tell by the color, size, or height of the body. Not by the color or size because the body had become burnt charcoal and not by the height because the two were of about the same height. So it remained to look for specific marks. The girl was a virgin and had never been pregnant nor given birth, while the servant was a married woman who had been pregnant and given birth, so one might be able to tell from the size and formation of the pelvis. This official doctor decided that it was the girl that had been burned and that the maid was the missing person, and the investigation was over.

It had happened while the doctor was carrying out his task and the investigator was examining the house that the *shaykh* suffered one of his severe but common fits and began to attack the doctor and the investigators. The investigator would have had him arrested except that the *'umda* intervened and whispered to him that the man was a *wali* and that the village had a strong belief in him and that he feared a popular disturbance if strong measures were taken against him. So they merely gave him a warning, and the doctor participated in this warning. He said angrily, "If you ever come to me, I will cut up your body with this scalpel." So the *shaykh* refrained from interfering and returned quietly to his place.

All of this left everyone dissatisfied.

In the first place, it was unthinkable that the girl should be burned when she was under the protection of the *shaykh*, and that the servant should be saved, even if they did not know where she was. Secondly, it was unthinkable that the doctor should threaten the *shaykh* and that the *shaykh* should not react and demonstrate his miraculous powers against him. It appears that during the course of his work the coroner had asked the barber-surgeon to help him. When he was told that there was a Sayyid al-Hakim in the town, he wanted to know who this person was and so he summoned him. When he found out that he was a former medical assistant, he employed him in place of the barber-surgeon.

From these elements there arose a long and extensive story that spread throughout the village quarters and survived for a long time, indeed lives on to the present moment. The story is that during the examination of the body there was an argument between the official doctor and Sayyid al-Hakim. The former decided that the one burned was the girl and the missing one was the servant, but the latter insisted that the one burned was the servant and the missing one was the girl. The official doctor, however, yelled at Sayyid al-Hakim not to question his words and so he was forced to keep silent, even though he knew he was right . . . most certainly right!

As for this shameless and reckless doctor who was ignorant of the *shaykh* and his powers, his finger had received a very small cut during the examination of the body just after the *shaykh* had left him. He had hardly arrived in Asyut when the wound became filled with pus, and they operated on him and cut off his finger. But the next day the pus had filled his forearm, so they performed another operation and amputated the forearm. But on the third day gangrene had filled his body and all of the doctors could do nothing to save him, so he died.

Thus the masses took revenge for their *shaykh* and restored his prestige, and satisfied the feelings of the girl's family and their strong hopes that their daughter was still alive.

Then what?

Then there arose unlimited fame for Sayyid al-Hakim, who had prevailed over the big doctor.

The servant was later found, a terrified and distraught fugitive owing to the severe fright she had suffered, but all of the people—and especially the girl's family—continued to believe that she was the girl, who had fled, whose face had turned black from shock, and whose tongue had become tied so that she could not speak clearly. If she had not died soon afterward, they would have made her heir to their possessions and included her in the family tree, because the *shaykh* could not be vanquished and Sayyid al-Hakim could not err.

This story has lived on in the village until now.

6   The 'Afarit

It was a moonlit night. Otherwise the boy and his small friends would
not have ventured out after sunset. They would not have sat calmly
on the mud-brick bench telling stories. And especially they would
not have sat in front of the old mill, which was famous for its 'afarit.[1]

The sun had just set and the evening meal was finished. The first
boys to come out went around to the houses of the others, calling to
them with pleasant-sounding songs, partly made up of intelligible
words and partly of mere rhythm and tune.

> Who doesn't come out and play
> The snake and the scorpion will bite.
> Even the snake charmer can't charm,
> Even the healer can't heal the harm.
> The tooth of a mouse,
> Near the herbalist's house,
> He beats the drum,
> Oh, how charming!

At every moment more children came out to join them. Whenever they passed by a house the children in it would hear the invita-
tion. They had no power to resist it and told their families that it was
absolutely necessary for them to go out, or else they would suffer

what the song threatened. The serpent, that is, the snake, or the scorpion would bite them, and neither the snake charmer nor the herbalist would be able to help them!

After they gathered they repaired to the bench, drawing confidence from the bright moon as it traveled through the sky. They were so entranced by the moonlight and the complete silence of the village that they became small, motionless phantoms listening to a story related by one of them while the rest were all ears. Suddenly a black tomcat jumped from the window of the small mill, and landed on the road near the bench and dashed off quickly. Dear reader, if ever you have watched as birds pecking seeds on the ground were surprised by a falcon swooping down from the sky or by a hunter taking aim at them, then you can imagine the sight of these youth as they ran away in terror at this sudden and terrifying apparition.

'Afarit!

This was the word they screamed out before they fled in terror, each one in the direction his feet happened to take him. All of them, that is, except Gomaa. Gomaa was a fat, simple, good-natured boy who had lost his mother. His house was near our friend's house and he was his dear childhood companion. There was a great difference between their families, because his grandmother was one of those who helped them with their housework, but that did not come between them nor disturb their innocent friendship.

Gomaa turned clumsy and his feet would not obey him, so he stammered and became agitated. The children's sudden movement had scared the tomcat so that it began to run to and fro. The poor boy reckoned that the 'ifrit was talking to him, and with that he finally lost his balance and fell down in a dead faint. Our friend observed his dear companion fall but in this situation he could not help him. Still, after he had run a considerable distance with his friends he looked about for his companion and did not see him, and then he felt a pressing urge to find out what had become of him. So he suggested to some of his friends that they return to search for their companion, whom they had left behind, and several of them responded, though with fear and trepidation. As they approached the site of the incident their courage almost deserted them, but desperation drove them on. Suddenly they came upon their companion, as still as a corpse but with some breath still in him. To no avail they attempted to arouse him. They stood for a long time at that terrifying spot before banding together to carry him to a safe place. His house was not far. They knocked at the door and his grandmother opened it to be confronted with the body of her grandson. She was troubled and alarmed, especially after she heard the story, and became convinced that the boy was possessed by an 'ifrit.

In the following days the poor grandmother attempted in vain to restore the health of her grandson with every available cure. She sprinkled water and salt about, from the bench upon which the 'afarit had descended all the way to the door of their house. She went to the awliya of the village and asked them to use their amulets and talismans to help her only grandson. She spent all of her meager savings to arrange a zar ceremony for him.[2] But none of these things had any effect. Day after day the child lost weight until, three months later, life finally departed from him.

Our friend walked in his companion's funeral procession, crying. It was the first funeral procession that he had ever attended. The whole event is etched in his mind and its memory cannot be erased. He did not return to the moonlit bench for three years, until he was ten years old, by which time he had attained a new belief concerning the 'afarit.

The mill was one of many old mills in the village. They were not mechanical or steam-powered but were of the simple, old-fashioned kind driven by animals, which, in the course of a day, could grind only a single measure of corn or a half-measure of wheat. These mills had been set up throughout the village before the child was born and the people were dependent upon them for grinding cereals. Usually cows drove them, although sometimes donkeys and camels were also employed. They were slow, noisy, and often dark. As a result, they overburdened both man and beast. These mills had largely fallen into disuse in later times when two steam-powered mills were set up in the village. But some of the villagers persevered in their belief that these modern machines spoiled the flour, and lacked *baraka*. They would not change the time-honored pattern of their life, and continued to run a few of the old-style mills. Among these was the "haunted" mill that the *'afarit* lived in.

The buildings of these ruined and abandoned mills remained and their desolation and idleness enhanced their wild appearance, especially during the numerous dark, moonless nights. It was then that the idea that they were "haunted" took hold, haunted by the worst *'afarit* that inhabited the village, who spread from there into some of the vacant houses and onto the dark, twisting pathways and blind alleys. They were thought to be especially prevalent at latrines.

Everything in the village inspired belief in the *'afarit*. When darkness covered the village after sunset, its streets became black; the person walking in them could not even see his feet and at every step was likely to bump into some unknown thing. The roads twisted like a snake's path, so that one never knew what was around any corner or beyond any curve, or whether it was safe or harmful. Hence, one approached every corner expecting some unknown danger. The naïve village imagination explained phenomena and events in terms of deeply rooted images and phantoms, frightening and mysterious in the dark gloom.

Then there were the *awliya* and the tales of their miracles spread by their followers, including examples of their ability to burn or bind the *'afarit*. The superstition of the *'afarit* mixes easily with the superstitions about the *awliya* because it links up in simple and ignorant souls with age-old beliefs about wonders and miracles and about the forces of good and evil in the universe.

In any case, the 'afarit were figures present in every mind and on every tongue, and were taken into account in people's every step and move, night or day. If a child fell on the floor, his mother, or whoever was present, would drop down to protect it and invoke the name of God. She would say to him: "You fell on your most beautiful sister" if the child was a boy, or, if it was a girl, "you fell on your most beautiful brother." This was done to flatter and appease the small female or male 'ifrit that the child had fallen upon. For it was thought that every woman had a qarina[3] or jinni "companion" and every time the female human gave birth to a boy, the female jinni gave birth to a girl and vice versa. Thus, if a child fell down, he fell on his counterpart. When this happened, one had on all accounts to flatter that jinni counterpart with the following saying: "You fell on your most beautiful sister," to avoid harm. This was to be accompanied by invoking the name of God, if one was a Muslim, or the name of the Virgin Mary and Jesus Christ if one was Christian. After that, one had to sprinkle the place with water and salt, which, they claimed, would terminate the evil between the sons of Adam and "our brothers," whom we dare not mention.

Although the logic of the superstition demanded that every person have a qarina of the opposite sex, this was not always the case, because the superstition also required every woman to have a female qarina. Like the woman, this qarina gives birth, matching every male born with a female. It happens in some cases that there is a beautiful male child who evokes the jealousy of the female qarina, because the latter has given birth to a girl only. Her jealousy of her female counterpart's beautiful son will increase until she finally strangles the child on the seventh night after its birth.

A brother of our child was, in fact, strangled by a qarina on the seventh night.[4] Our friend's mother strove to provide him with a brother who would give him support and companionship. He picked up on his mother's hope and identified with it even though he himself did not know its true meaning. Then God heard his mother's prayer and the prayers of her friends. In this way, God had fulfilled the prophecy of Shaykh Bakr whom one of these friends had visited, inquiring about her friend's burden. The *shaykh* had given this friend a stick of sugarcane, which symbolized the coming of a male child.

The birth of a healthy baby boy enhanced the joy and harmony of the family, and it made ready to celebrate the seventh day of the child's birth with a *mawlid*, at which musicians would sing and professional reciters read from the Qur'an. Sweetmeats would be handed out to family and neighbors and food distributed to the poor. But as all of this was being planned, the newborn baby began on the sixth day to display strange symptoms, which, little by little, developed into a nervous fit that almost suffocated him. The baby frothed and foamed at the mouth and turned dark or even black. Just as the suffering appeared to be unbearable, the fit would subside and the baby would settle down, until it seized him again. There was no doubt about it: It was the *qarina*. The beauty and health of the child had vexed her, filling her with envy of the family, so that she began to strangle the baby.

People looked to the *awliya* for a solution. Although his father did not, for the most part, believe in the *awliya* or in the *qarina*, he experienced the weakness that all humans feel in the presence of danger, especially danger to life. He wanted the newborn to live and if it died, did not want to bear the responsibility for its death in the eyes of its mother.

All of these factors, combined with the traces of these superstitions that reason could not erase from his mind, prompted him to agree to this course of action. Because the baby's mother was still recovering from childbirth and was distraught over the baby's precarious condition, it was left to his aunt to take him to the *awliya*, both living and dead. It was hoped that they would be able to save his threatened life from the vengeful *qarina*, which continued to strangle him until he was in sight of death and then left him alone for a moment because of the *baraka* of the amulets, charms, and spells, which calmed and pacified him.

But something happened that nullified hope in the baby's recovery and almost took his aunt's life too. It was a moonlit night and it was a short distance between her house and that of her sister, the baby's mother. So it occurred to her, as she was taking the baby to the *wali's* house in the dead of night, to pass by her house to see if her own aunt would accompany her. Now, her aunt was a blessed lady and a relative of the *wali* she intended to visit. The house was in a long, winding alley in the middle of which was a well with a trough from which the animals drank and next to it was a date palm belonging to one of the houses.

Because it was a moonlit night, shadows were cast in every direction, and that of the palm, swaying in the wind, reflected on the moonlit ground. Whenever the palm moved, its shadow lengthened and then shortened. Unavoidably the aunt was already in a state of fright, because she was convinced that the child she carried on her shoulders was pursued by a *qarina* who was intent on strangling him to death. She was alone in the dark night, and it appeared to her that there was a terrifying ghost that lengthened and shortened and swayed left and right. The leaves of the palm appeared as fearful whips in the hands of this ghost about to pounce on her. That was enough to unhinge her but she gathered all her strength and ran on in terror, until she reached the door of the house. She knocked at the door violently and fearfully, waking up those who were sleeping inside. She then fell down on the doorstep, clasping the baby in her hands, still as death!

Then she recovered and was able to go with her aunt and a man from her family to the house of the *wali*. She went for the sake of the newborn, mainly, but also for her own sake. But the *wali* refused to see them. And that signaled the failure of the mission and the fulfillment of destiny.

On the seventh day, during one of the acute attacks, the newborn gasped his last breath. Tetanus had overcome him as a result of the nonsterile knife used by the midwife to cut the umbilical cord. The tetanus microbe clung to it, causing the wound to be infected. There it remained for the duration of its incubation period, which ranges between four to six days. With that, the *qarina* had accomplished her mission, venting her fury at the beautiful baby boy.

From that day our child wore an amulet that had originally belonged to a Maghribi gypsy. It was a rare amulet because it bore an image of Our Lord Solomon that offered protection against Iblis and all of his sons, and the *qarina* and all her daughters, forbidding these from causing harm to its wearer. He continued to wear the amulet until he came to another understanding about the *'afarit* as a result of the education he gained at school. He finally rid himself of the amulet when God fulfilled his mother's hope for another child. It was bestowed upon the newborn from the first day, and because of that the *qarina* was not able to do the baby any harm. And so he lived and eventually graduated from university. I do not know what my brother thinks today about the amulet that saved his life; I cannot coax from him any memory of those days.[5]

How did he come by this new belief, which defied the beliefs of the villagers? The story is as follows.

Dozens of stories and images about *'afarit* were poured into his ears and mind. In the old mill, for example, was an *'ifrit* that appeared in the form of a black cat, whose curse no one was able to survive. The incident involving his friend Gomaa was unquestioned evidence of this. Other mills were operated at night by *'afarit* when no one was around. Passersby could hear the mills operating, along with the crack of the whip that the driver used on the back of the bull, "ha! Ha!" At other sites the *muzayyara* would appear. She was an *'ifrit* who took the form of a tall woman attired in the *tazyira*, which is a special black dress, covered by a shawl that is dyed and starched. One could hear the rustling sounds caused by her movements. She clasped a torch with which she burned anyone she saw. At the deserted well in the middle of the village appeared a woman with disheveled hair, sweeping with a broom in circles around the well. Woe to anyone who dared approach her after the evening prayer! On a dark stretch on one of the roads a woman was seen walking and then squatting down, as though she were looking for something on the ground. The Nile also had its mermaid-like jinn. When the Nile overflowed and flooded its banks, it teemed with these jinn, who would appear especially to the young men as they swam in the channel, but would shortly sweep out of sight and disappear in the water.

Then there was that traditional *'ifrit* who appeared on the paths of the fields in the form of a fat lamb, with no shepherd or owner in sight. This tempted the one who found it to take it to his house. As they approached the lamb, it would suddenly turn and say, "Take me back to where you found me," or, according to other versions, it would grow in size as it repeated these words, or else turn into a small child as it repeated the demand. That is when the man would realize that he was confronting an *'ifrit*. At such a point God might inspire him to recite something from the Qur'an, al-Samadiyya or the verse of The Throne,[6] at which point the *'ifrit* would disappear in flames. Or, if he should know the Greatest Name of God, that name known only to a small elite and divulged only with special permission, that was enough to chain the *'ifrit* and nail it fast to the ground, subjugating it and making it submissive, fearing the approach of dawn. It would then begin to ingratiate itself with the bearer of the Greatest

Name, until he would relent and let it go. If the man who took the calf did neither, then woe upon woe to him.

Similar to the tradition of the lamb is one pertaining to a donkey, which some people might come across on one of the paths leading to the fields. He would be saddled and would have a bridle in his mouth, and thus fitted would lure people to ride him. The one who mounted him was fated to fall into a devilish trap. Then things would proceed as with the lamb, with the addition that the donkey would rise up in the air with its rider on top screaming for help. If he did not know the Greatest Name of God, or if he was ignorant of the Qur'an, or was not able at that moment to recall anything of it, he would be thrown to the ground and descend to the seventh region of Hell, or, at the very least, dismount as a complete wreck.

'Afarit were everywhere. Everything that set foot on the ground at night or whose shadow appeared in the moonlight was an 'ifrit stalking the passersby, who, wherever they went, were always in fear. Some 'afarit were even so bold as to show up in broad daylight in the form of black cats. Therefore, it was forbidden to strike a black cat during the day, or any cat at night, because it might be an 'ifrit or else the soul of one of those humans whose souls could roam apart from their bodies.

The stories of the roaming souls were as well known as those of the 'afarit. The souls of some children, especially twins, were believed to roam freely when they were asleep, that is, they left the body and were usually or always seen in the form of a cat. If this cat were confined for any reason, the child whose soul it was remained asleep and never woke. And if the cat were beaten, the child became sick and sensed pain in the area of the body corresponding to where the cat was struck. He finally died if the soul-bearing cat was killed. Therefore, for fear of a cat's being an 'ifrit, it was forbidden to strike cats at night, and people were warned against doing so during the day.

Comparable to the cat representing a soul, there was a green fly that resembled a small bee, which was also thought to be a soul. People believed that this was one of the souls of the dead that flew about the houses, around family and friends, generating in their hearts feelings of sociability. Naturally, it was forbidden to harm them or to eject them from the house.

But the most devilish and shocking act of boldness on the part of the 'afarit took place when they rushed into some of the mosques. Yet, despite their courage, they dared not enter the prayer room, but confined their presence to the lavatory. My uncle, Shaykh 'Ali, was once involved in an incident. He was a man who followed the straight path, whose beard jutted out in front and whose turban was long at the back. It happened one morning that he was awakened early by the crowing of a rooster. He made his way to the mosque, assuming that it was time for the early-morning prayer, when in fact it was only a little past midnight. Once there, he went to perform his ablutions and opened the faucet. Then something flowed onto his hands, not water but fresh meat that took the shape of a child! But he was a man who knew God's Greatest Name. He was self-confident and felt secure against the 'afarit. So he was patient in the face of this troublesome joke and said to the 'ifrit, "Go and may God ease your path." He then shifted to another faucet, and a third, and a fourth, and the episode was repeated. When he cried out the Greatest Name of God, the 'ifrit emitted a deafening shout and said to him, "I am but a small child, release me, Sir." Compassion overtook the shaykh and he smiled and released him for the sake of God.

Many children were "exchanged." This happened when a small child was alone in a frightening place such as a lavatory, when the 'ifrit would appear and kidnap the human child and put in his place a jinni child. The child was returned only after long procedures, such as plunging into the Nile and uttering, "Take your child and give us back ours," until this was finally done.

There is one full month when people were given rest from the 'afarit and the constant fear that pursued them in their daily activities. It was a time when adults and children felt free to visit one another in their homes and stay up late without fear, playing in the streets and in the fields. It was a time when women got up in the middle of the night to do their work, especially the preparation of dough for baking at dawn. This was the month of Ramadan, during which all of the 'afarit, whether small or fully grown, are chained and are out of the view of humans. This has been so since the age of Solomon, may peace be upon him!

Because dozens of these images, myths, and accounts were constantly being impressed on his young mind, how could he ever have been able to change his beliefs about the 'afarit? Yet this happened when a young headmaster came to the school. He was deeply concerned about the moral and spiritual education of the students and did not simply limit himself to dry scholastic subjects. When he saw how the myth of the 'afarit occupied a solid place in the perceptions and feelings of the students, he tried as much as he could to purify their minds of it.

He said to them, "All talk about these 'afarit is superstition based on ignorance, and all the tales about those who unexpectedly encountered 'afarit are fabricated for some ulterior purpose, or else are simply imagined. The cats, dogs, and other animals that many people think are 'afarit are in fact real animals. Fear and dread create these thoughts in people, especially since they meet them in the dark, where they cannot see forms clearly." He made this subject the focus of conversation in many of his classes, until some of the students were almost at the point of believing what he said.

Our friend trusted and loved this headmaster. He believed him and was influenced by him. But the 'afarit! They resided too deeply in his feelings to be erased even by all of these arguments, although the basis for belief in them was indeed shaken in his soul. It took an actual incident, or a number of such, to demolish these beliefs and to establish new ones in their place. Circumstances gave the teacher the opportunity to see that such incidents took place.

Some of the students said to him, "There are 'afarit that appear in the form of rabbits in the narrow alley after midnight." The reputation of this narrow alley for 'afarit was at least equivalent to the notorious haunted mill. This alley originated with a house that was built in the middle of the village between two roads. The owner decided that he had no need for the house and so opened a path through it that connected the two roads. This saved a considerable distance for those who needed to go from one road to the other. Just two passageways had been opened through the house, while its roofs and courtyards remained dark, even during the day. It was here that the 'afarit lived. The alley became a source of terror for those who walked it, so that even some men were afraid to traverse it alone during the day. Children were even more afraid. At night the mark of greatest courage was for someone to pass though it alone, and rarely did anyone risk such an outrageous adventure.

So when the teacher was told that 'afarit appeared in the ally after midnight, he seized the opportunity and asked some of the students to accompany him at night, at an agreed time, to see these rabbits, capture one of them, and examine it. Here the students wavered between fear and curiosity. The presence of the headmaster, whose abilities they trusted, in addition to the protective verses of the Qur'an they had memorized for just such occasions, emboldened them. Six of them volunteered to undertake the dangerous experiment. Naturally our friend was one of them.

Before the set time they gathered at the school to launch the first mission of its kind in the village. So when the time came, and traffic on the roads had ceased except for the watchmen, the intrepid campaigners set out for the narrow alley and the dreaded lair of the 'afarit.

As they approached, their knees began to quake and their hearts to tremble. Each one of them searched his memory for the Qur'anic verses al-Samadiyya and The Throne to fortify and strengthen himself. Reassuring words flowed from the headmaster, although, in fact, they had no effect. Then the mission plunged into the lair with the headmaster in the lead. Here the experiment almost failed and brought about results exactly contrary to its purpose.

The students confronted numerous eyes, red and blue, glowing in the dark. The eyes of the 'afarit, no doubt, sparking with evil, just as they had so often heard. These were the 'ifrit-rabbits, leaping and jumping, running from here to there, passing between their legs and brushing by them in every direction. They began to waver and lost all the determination and cohesiveness that had been instilled in them. The protective verses of the Qur'an slipped their memories and so were lost to them. This is the greatest danger facing those who confront the 'afarit, because in the confusion of battle they lose their only weapon. This all had lasted for only a moment when they heard the headmaster call out, "These are rabbits! Just rabbits! Don't be afraid! They belong to the owners of the nearby houses. Catch one of them so we can take a look at it. Capture it and don't be afraid. Surround it so we can catch it."

Some of the trust that had been shaken from their hearts returned. The headmaster had managed to catch one of the rabbits and so he announced that the mission had ended successfully and they should return to their bases safely with their prize. In vain he tried to encourage one of the students to hold the rabbit for a moment. But who would be mad enough to grasp the 'ifrit in his hands? Therefore they returned to the school and with each step they expected the 'ifrit to cry out and beseech them to return him to his place, otherwise woe to them all. Or, perhaps, he would transform himself in the hands of the headmaster into a cat or dog, or else vanish from his hands into thin air without his realizing it. But the rabbit form did not change into an 'ifrit nor even utter a word. Thus they returned to school, where tranquility reigned. Who knows? Maybe the headmaster was right in what he said, after all.

Right or wrong, they would not allow it to spend the night with any one of them, as the headmaster suggested. For who knows, the 'ifrit might appear to be peaceful in this way because they are a group? But when alone with one of them he might behave like an 'ifrit once again. It was decided that they would keep the 'ifrit overnight at the school and come in the morning to see him. If they found him there, he was really a rabbit. But if they did not find him, or found another animal in his place, he was really an 'ifrit.

The experiment worked. Dawn came and they found a genuine rabbit. The headmaster sent the school's caretaker to ask at the homes nearby the narrow alley if anyone had lost a rabbit. He returned with the son of a resident who claimed the missing rabbit, the same rabbit that had escaped under the door into the narrow alley, as he did every night with his brother rabbit-'afarit!

The experiment, no doubt, had its value, but it was not decisive, and at least one more experiment was needed before the belief in 'afarit was shaken. The headmaster had been told that there was a woman with loose disheveled hair who appeared on some nights at the deserted well in the middle of the village. She swept the ground as she sat and moved around the well in a circular fashion. He agreed with a number of the students that they should capture this female 'ifrit. What daring! But why not try it, especially as they had returned from their first experiment safe and sound?

Night after night, when the streets were deserted, they walked around the well but were unable to spot the jinni in question. But that did not stop them from attempting the experiment again and again until one night they were successful. But who would step forward to face the danger this time, because not every time is one able to escape unscathed. Their bold headmaster stepped forward, though even he hesitated to come too close. But once he realized that his reluctance and confusion would destroy everything that he had built up in the students, he took courage and approached, aided by a box of matches that lit the way.

What did he find?

An old woman, muttering in disgust, "Leave me alone, child, so that I can sweep the road for the Pasha director." What director? What road? This vagueness gave rise to fear and doubt. But they noticed the door ajar in the house and they realized what the situation was. She was a senile woman well known to the village. The visit of the Pasha director to the village years earlier had been a unique and awesome occasion and had stirred up the whole village, because every homeowner had been obliged to sweep in front of his house and sprinkle it with water. She still remembered this event, which had fixed itself in her mind, and she imagined that she still had to sweep the road for him.

The rabbits in the narrow alley, the woman at the abandoned well, these, along with his beloved teacher's instruction, had their influence on our child. He was now ten years old and had almost completed his primary schooling. The myth of the 'afarit was losing something of its power over his mind. It was further shaken to the extent that he was able to perform his own experiments. This was great progress.

He would walk around with a box of matches always in his pocket, even though he did not smoke, for he had seen how the matches had saved the day in the case of the woman at the well. Thus he adopted the laudable habit and always carried this weapon with him. He was all the more encouraged to do this when he heard that the 'afarit fear light and would not oppose anyone who could stand up to them firmly and unflinchingly when he encountered them.

He used to traverse the village streets after the evening prayer (he had by then started to pray in the mosque like the men). Since the time he had turned ten he imagined himself as a responsible man of special importance, and so it would not be proper for him to abstain from praying in congregation with the men. Also, he began to stay up late at night, even, sometimes, until ten o'clock. Was he not a man? So why shouldn't he stay up late as the men do? This meant that he had to return home in the dark and pass by the dwelling places of the 'afarit, which were scattered throughout the village. Not one road was free of one or two hideouts. When he approached one of these lairs, his knees would tremble and his heart would race. He found that he was not able to go past it, fearing that the 'ifrit might allow him to go by and then pursue him. In this case, he preferred to approach the hideout and enter it. He would then light a match and stand to inspect every nook and cranny of the place. He would even look through the keyhole in the door of the old mill and other such places as well, in order to be more certain. Once he felt sure there was nothing there, he would proceed down the road feeling semi-secure, until he reached another lair. And the process would repeat itself.

He was in an extraordinary state during this period. He was trying not to believe in 'afarit and would screw up his courage to walk in the dark right by their hideouts, so dreaded by everyone else. Yet at the same time he was afraid and still stopped to investigate them. He deluded himself into thinking that he was free of that cursed myth. People found out that he purposefully walked by these danger spots, and some of them worried about him while others admired him. This admiration encouraged him to carry his experiments even further. From that day on he never came across even one of the many 'afarit that hindered passersby everywhere as they made their way.

As I say, he did not come across one 'ifrit. But the truth is that one night he almost lost all of the confidence that the various incidents had built up in him over time. He had then turned eleven and had been invited with the other members of his family to his cousin's wedding. They were supposed to remain there until about midnight and then return home. But it appeared that his mother had forgotten one of her belongings at their house and wanted someone to fetch it for her. Our friend volunteered to undertake the mission with all the gallantry of a man. But his mother was afraid to send him alone, and her fear hurt his pride. And so he insisted on making the trip and returning alone. There were two roads leading from his aunt's house to his own. One of these was a long road that skirted the edges of the village. The other road was shorter but passed through the narrow alley. His mother warned against taking this shortcut.

This warning was enough to make him rush to the short route at that late hour, and in the village it is considered to be late when the men have returned from their evening prayers. Although he felt terrified as he came to the alley, he still went in. And there something happened that stirred up the fear that lay hidden behind his precarious courage. In one of the corners of the house that comprised the alley there was a stack of baked bricks. As he drew near to it he sensed a movement that made the stack wobble and heard the sound of the brick molds knocking together. Then he glanced and noticed a glow peeping between the cracks of the large stack. At that moment he took out his weapon and lit a match. Calm returned and the glow vanished. Then the flame went out and the motion returned.

He almost lost his resolve when he repeated the process several times with the same result. His feet were pinned to the ground. He no longer dared confront the danger, and could not leave this dangerous place. Time passed and he feverishly continued to light the matches until they were nearly exhausted. He could go neither forward nor backward nor stop lighting the matches. Then God's providence came to his rescue. The alternating light and darkness startled a man who was passing by. Fearful, he advanced cautiously until he noticed, at the moment our friend lit one of the matches, a human face. In a frightened voice he called out, "man or jinn?" The child recovered and told the man his name.

The man drew near to him, astonished and perplexed. Our friend lit the last match and the man asked with evident concern, "What brought you here, my son, at such a late hour? God has protected you."

His superficial courage returned to him and he replied, "I am not afraid. I do not believe what is said about these 'afarit! I was just standing here investigating about these 'afarit that they speak of."

He learned afterwards that a group of mice was living in that stack of bricks, and it was their eyes that glowed in the dark. They had become quiet and the glow in their eyes disappeared when the match was struck.

Days passed. He left everything in the village and lived his life in the city and broadened his education. The myth of the 'afarit became a source of amusement and jest. But inquire of his dreams and visions today. They will tell you that the myth of the 'afarit is more deeply embedded in his soul than education, and that the 'afarit that inhabited his mind in childhood and youth will inhabit his imagination forever.

7   Cultural Activity

For three or four days during certain months of the year, an event occurred in the village that captured the interest of those among its inhabitants who could read and whose fond memory would continue until the time for it came round again. Those were the days when Uncle Salih would arrive in the village, carrying a sack filled with books over his shoulder. After emptying the sack he would sit cross-legged on it in the village's small marketplace, arranging the books, some twenty or thirty of them, in front of him in rows according to their value or their subject matter.

Mind, reader, that you do not smile as I describe for you this "library" stacked on the ground, for its contents and diverse topics deserve your respect. There were books of *shu'r*, as we children pronounced it. The educated men in the village also pronounced it this way to distinguish it from the *sh'ir*, the proper poetry of the Arabs of olden times, which we used to memorize at school. Among these were the many different stories of 'Abu Zayd, the stories of al-Zir Salim and Kulayb, and the stories of Zaynati Khalifa and Diyab Ibn Ghanim.[1]

Among the panegyrics and biographies you could find the *Burda*, and works of Sidi Ibrahim al-Desuqi, Sayyid al-Badawi, and Bint Bari, and Sidi 'Abd al-Qadir al-Jilani. Also to be found were the works of Sa'd al-Yatim and the book *Information on the Fate of the Barmakids at the*

Hands of the Abbasids.[2] The section on heroes included books of Amira Dhat al-Himma, "the Hero" Sidi Muhammad, and Queen Hannah.[3] Found also were religious books, such as *Dala'il al-Khayrat* and Prayers for mid-Sha'ban and for Laylat al-Qadr.[4]And there were detective stories: *Sherlock Holmes*, *Sinclair*, and the *Noble Thief*. In the general culture section you could find books on the subject of education and moral training. You could also find the first section of the grammar book by the late Hamza Fath Allah,[5] or the book entitled *Marvels of Blooms in the Circumstances of Fortune*.

Sometimes it happened that Uncle Salih's sack contained what were considered to be the most dangerous books of all: Copies of *'Antar the Knight*[6] and *A Thousand and One Nights*. Or—and here I must ask, reader, that you whisper these words to yourself—Abu Ma'shar al-Falaki's book on astrology,[7] the book of Shamhurish on magic, and the book *Fara'id al-Tibiyya* on medicine. Uncle Salih disclosed these books only to select customers and readers. And he would not hand them over to these customers unless they gave him their solemn oath that they would not use them to harm people. These books, therefore, had a special magical quality. The exchange would be carried out in the same manner as the most weighty pacts and secret agreements.

Our friend was an excellent customer of Uncle Salih, who knew him well and reserved for him the best and most dangerous books. In return, our friend did not spare any expense for these books, however much they might cost, even spending as much as five piastres at one time. These valuable books started out at one millieme and went up to two piastres. They rarely cost any more unless they belonged to the last category of secret and dangerous books.

The three or four days that Uncle Salih would spend in the village were the most beautiful of days for our friend. He saved up for them by cutting down on what he spent, and if he ran out of funds he would turn to his father and ask him for one, two, or sometimes even five piastres. That was a huge amount of money in those days, seeing as he was no more than ten years old and lived in a village where there were few opportunities to spend the small allowance he got from his father. All his needs for fruits and sweets were met, except when he wanted to buy sugarcane from Uncle Khalil, and he was forbidden to acquire poor-quality dates and unripe apples. His father acquired for the house the best of these fruits that the village could provide. He did not dare take anything from the storage room or from the house, though petty thievery was tolerated in other houses, as we shall see. Thus five piastres was not a trivial amount of money in those days. Even so, he would hand all of it over in one transaction for these books. It is no wonder, then, that Uncle Salih should have regarded him as one of his favorite customers.

He had friends—readers like him—who were also customers of Uncle Salih. Some of them were students at the school and some were youth who had graduated or left when their moustaches sprouted and their beards grew, and so were considered to be men.

He and his friends sought Uncle Salih's company during the three active days. They bought from him what their budgets allowed and, for a deposit of one millieme, they could read other books that interested them so long as they did so right there beside Uncle Salih in the corner of the market. This applied to everyone except our friend. He was allowed to take any book home with him in return for a half-piastre deposit. He would return it if he was not willing to buy it or if his budget was not sufficient for its purchase. In the latter case he would make Uncle Salih promise to keep the book for him until he returned, by which time our friend would have saved up the prodigious sum needed. When Uncle Salih returned he would always have kept his promise!

This cultural activity did not stop upon Uncle Salih's departure. The readers exchanged among themselves the books that they had purchased until everyone had read them. By then the time for his return would be near and they would begin to wait for him. Thus it went throughout the year.

Our friend was famous among the cultured people of the village for his books and reading habits. He was respected in their eyes and they predicted a glorious future for him. Why? Had he not, even at his young age, acquired a large library, so enormous that it filled an entire tin chest?

Yes, a tin chest. That is what Uncle Salih advised him to get. He told him that wood "breeds" moths and cockroaches, but tin does not. The chest could, on occasion, easily be wiped with petrol to deter these insects from getting too close to it. Thus, being protective of his books, he had obtained this tin chest for them and had had the local tinsmith prepare a tight tin cover for it. Therefore his library was protected and grew and grew until it eventually contained twenty-five books. In fact, he was passionately fond of this library, which was unique in the village by virtue of its diverse contents. All it lacked to make it comprehensive was a copy of al-Bukhari's *hadith* collection.[8]

But where could a child like him acquire a copy of al-Bukhari? Those that existed were in the possession of the approximately ten Azharis who lived in the village, and who enjoyed a position of great prestige. Everyone kissed their hands as though they were *awliya*. In fact, the only people in the village who enjoyed more prestige than these scholars were the *magzubs* and the *awliya*.*

These men possessed al-Bukhari, and so did two others in the village, two preachers, that is, Qur'an reciters, who also, however, prac-

---

*Author's note: This was a quarter-century ago. Today there are more than one hundred in the village who have undertaken intermediate or higher studies or have gone to teachers' colleges.

ticed magic and engaged in the weaving of spells and the fashioning
of amulets and talismans. The ill child, the insane woman, the rejected wife, and the "bound man" who is put under a spell on his wedding night so that he is deprived of his manhood until the bond of the
spell is lifted: all of these got from these two men, and from many
other practitioners of "writing"—that is, the writing of magic spells—
what they sought in return for a recognized fee. What distinguished
these two men from the others is the fact that each owned a copy of
al-Bukhari, which otherwise were only in the possession of scholars
coming from the Azhar in Cairo.

So why did a copy of al-Bukhari hold such value? It often happened that when homes were robbed, the perpetrator was the lady of
the house, the son's wife, one of the sons, or one of the servants. The
objects of such theft were items such as food that was stored in the
house or barn, a piece of gold, or money.

It was well known that house servants might steal. But why would
the sons or their wives or the lady of the house do such a thing? The
explanation can be found in the economic arrangements. After the
sons grew up and got married, which they did, of course, following
the example of their parents, their fathers would continue to support
them and their wives for many years until the fathers died and they
inherited his wealth, but the fathers would fail to recognize how
much the sons needed for their day-to-day expenses. Thus, as a boy
grew up and became a young man, he had no alternative but to steal
in order to have money to spend with his friends. He had to pay his
share of the cost of the sugarcane they enjoyed together. He had to
buy either the tea they drank or the sugar to go with it. He had to
contribute for the meat they bought together and ate secretly in a
field or in one of their houses. Therefore the amount the young men
got from their families was not enough for their needs at this stage
of life.

For this reason a young man had to steal, and also for other reasons. He might be engaged to be married and would have to give presents to his fiancée and her family in addition to the few presents his family gave her. His presents might include a heavily embroidered handkerchief, two pounds of grapes, a quarter-kilo of dates, or a bundle of twenty-four stalks of sugarcane. These and other gifts cost money, money that a young man could not obtain without stealing from his father's house throughout his engagement. And this continued into the period of the honeymoon, when the husband was required to obtain for his wife, behind the backs of his mother and father, quantities of mixed nuts, sweets, candy, and bathing soap, in amounts greater than what was usually found in the village houses.

His wife also had a hand in these thefts. She was young and had demands that conflicted with the generally tight-fisted requirements of the household. She needed embroidered scarves, scented soap, and bottles of perfumes that would please her young husband. She also needed combs made of bone, such as the itinerant vendors carried, which she would show off to the women and especially the younger ones when she went visiting. This was particularly during the early days of marriage. She also stole because her ripening young body required different sorts of nutritional foods that were not usually available to her at home. During the first days of marriage her own family provided her with these foods. Every day of the first week they would bring what is called the "big dinner," consisting of either a full or half goat or lamb and a pot or two of cooked vegetables. It also included *mishmishiyya*, which is dried apricot cooked in water, sugar, and clarified butter. All of this was offered to the groom's family. The newlyweds received a sufficient portion of this same food, called the "small dinner," except that it was of a higher quality than the "big dinner" and had a greater quantity of clarified butter. In an open display, all of the girls and women, each carrying a pot, would carry this dinner from the home of the bride to the house of the groom's family after the afternoon prayer.

After the first week people differed in their practice of sending the "big dinner" and the "small dinner." Some would send over the big dinner once every week and the small dinner every day for a month, then they would stop sending the big dinner while the small dinner would continue for a time. This period would vary in length depending on their financial condition and generosity. The villagers would remember all this and talk about it for some years, or perhaps indefinitely.

But all of this would come to an end toward the end of the first year of marriage at the latest. The bride was still young and her body needed more than the food shared with her by the family of the house, and so she would inevitably resort to stealing from behind the backs of her in-laws in order to make up for the lack in her nutrition. She would get the woman who sold shanks, hearts, livers, kidneys, and stomachs to secretly set aside a suitable amount on Mondays and Thursdays—the days on which the livestock in the village was slaughtered—and then to cook these at home for her and then bring them to her, claiming that it was her family that had sent her this extra food, which could be either meat or these different kinds of organs. Or she would have the woman give it to her raw and she would cook it secretly at night in her own room and she and her young husband would share a surreptitious meal.

The lady of the house would also steal, either because she had the same needs as her daughter-in-law or because she wanted to put aside something for herself or else provide something for her son's engagement expenses beyond what his father gave him. Some of the heads of households discovered these thefts in their homes, but chose to be silent. These were the wise and generous ones. They knew the needs of their sons and their wives and knew that they were not satisfying their demands. So they kept quiet. Even so, they did not attempt to satisfy these demands so as to end these thefts. Others, however, would rage, shout, and make threats, interrogating the various members of the family, as well as the servants and some visitors. Of course, everyone would deny the charge. This is where al-Bukhari came in.

The suspects were able to swear falsely by God and His Prophet and yet feel safe. But there were other oaths that they dared not take, for if they lied there would descend upon them unavoidable misfortune. The first of these oaths, which no one dared to take, was the injunction to place one's hand on a copy of the Qur'an, close one's eyes, and then swear that he did not commit the offense in question. There was another oath that was even stronger: the *"shuri"* vow, in which the defendant would say, "By my *'shuri'* I did not commit this." If he lied he would suffer the consequences and inevitably become blind, suffer a fracture, or even experience an incurable disease. Stronger still than the *"shuri"* vow was to swear by one of the *awliya*. These varied greatly. Some could not bear an oath uttered falsely in their name and would punish the offender promptly by appearing to him in a dream and either warning him or giving him a beating. Usually the man would rise from his sleep in terror, admit his guilt, and beg forgiveness. Other *awliya* were patient and would give the offender more or less time, but by no means would leave him alone indefinitely, especially if he had placed his hand on the dome of the *shaykh's* tomb.

But the most fearsome oath of all, the one that shook people's nerves, was used only when the person was confident of his innocence or anxious to meet his fate. This was the oath over al-Bukhari. From the moment the thief laid his hand on the text of al-Bukhari and closed his eyes, his body would tremble and shiver, his heartbeat would rise and fall, and he would show signs of utter terror. He would then either confess at once, or refuse to take the oath so that the refusal would prove his guilt. If he dared actually to take the oath, then he would last but three days until al-Bukhari would take effect and he would suffer his fate, which would likely be mental confusion and a nervous breakdown that would usually lead to death or insanity.

There were special customs and rituals associated with the al-Bukhari oath. The owner of the text had to take it into the home that was robbed, or else have the suspects brought to his own house for the administration of the oath, in exchange for a recognized fee.

Yes, there were other ways to identify the thief, namely, the "mandal" method and the "cup" method. The mandal was a small pitcher filled with water, which the soothsayer held by a cord attached to its neck. All of the suspects would sit around him in a circle. Then he would begin to recite magic incantations and spells over the mandal and burn special incense. He would then move the pitcher from person to person, holding it by the cord and shaking it. The water would spill from its spout as it passed the thief, thus silently identifying him. The "cup" method involved a small child who would be brought in and hypnotized. He would hold a cup with coffee grounds in his hands while the soothsayer recited spells and incantations. He would command him to look into the bottom of the cup to see if there were any activity, whether of men or women. These latter would be a group of jinn who had appeared in order to serve and were thus called "servants." The soothsayer would tell the boy to order these jinn to sweep and sprinkle the floor with water and to arrange the chairs. And the boy would see the jinn do just that. He would ask the boy to order the jinn to summon the thief. The boy would see the jinn bring forward a certain man or woman and would be asked by the soothsayer to say who this person resembled. By now exhausted, the boy would mention the name of someone whom he knew. The boy would then dismiss the servants and fall into a deep sleep.[9]

Thus the thief was identified. In fact, however, most of the time he would have already confessed to the soothsayer once he learned that the "cup" or mandal was to be employed. But neither the mandal nor the cup had the same potency as al-Bukhari. Therefore, the al-Bukhari oath remained unique. Perhaps you now understand how very valu-

able it was under these circumstances for at least one of the people to
have a copy.

It was not given to our friend to have a copy of al-Bukhari in his
great library. He was not a scholar from the Azhar, nor was he a
preacher like the two preachers who were famous throughout the village for their Bukharis and their ability to cast spells, in particular
spells for wives over their husbands or over their co-wives, spells to
make men impotent or to release them from it, and spells against enemies in general, causing sickness and madness. Many in the village,
both then and now, had been enchanted in these ways.

But if he could not have a copy of al-Bukhari, he still had other
books in his library that earned him, at his young age, great fame and
celebrity in the village, especially among the women but also among
a group of the youth. He had in his library two books: one by 'Abu
Ma'shar al-Falaki and the other by Shamhurish. Each was related to a
story that helped to spread his fame:

The book by 'Abu Ma'shar al-Falaki comprised a number of chapters and dealt with astrology. Of note was one chapter devoted to different fortunes meted out to people born in certain months, seasons,
and days. Also of interest was a chapter devoted to discerning a
person's fortune from the letters of his name, his mother's name, and
the name of the month in which he was born, and adding them together by a well-known system, used by some numerologists
throughout history, in which each letter corresponds to a number.
The letter *alif* was equivalent to the number one, *ba* was equivalent to
two, *jim* to three, in the following order of the letters: *abajad, buwwaz,
hatti, kalamun, sa'afas, qursht*.[10] The tenth letter is *ta*, with an equivalency
of ten, the *ya* is twenty, and the *kaf* thirty. At the end of the second ten
was *qaf*. Then began the one hundred series with the *ra* as two hun-

dred, and so on. If I remember correctly, this reckoning is taken from the ancient Hebrew language. There was another chapter in the book that instructed a person who sought to find out more about his future to place his finger on a page filled with different numbers. The number chosen represented a specific page in the chapter in which was written his past, present, and future fortunes. Also written was information about his personal traits, his character, his adversaries, his loved ones, and other things about him, as well as what he needed to do, what he ought to watch out for, and so forth.

As for Shamhurish's book, it contained many spells, incantations, and charms, and recipes for incense. Some brought love and others brought happiness. And some gave one access to rulers so as to be received with respect and granted one's needs.

The women and young people of the village heard about these two books and so approached our small friend avidly. And they did so for several reasons. One reason was that he did not require payment for the services that he provided for them. Another was the fact that he was young and could enter houses without causing problems. In contrast to the presence of adults who practiced the profession, he could enter houses without raising questions in people's minds the way older practitioners of this profession would. Still another reason was that a woman or girl would not be embarrassed to confess their secret desires and fears to a boy who had not yet reached the age of puberty. Some of these factors were in the minds of the young people, so most of the jobs given to him were confidential ones of this sort.

He would return from school to find requests to meet with him from a number of houses. Some even sent a messenger to wait for him and take him to the client, especially after it became widely known that he was busy with many such missions. The truth is that he felt a strange delight at all these requests. All doors were opened to him. He was young, and sexual impulses had not yet begun to stir in him.

Even if they had, his upbringing at home had instilled in him a great deal of modesty. Still, his sensitivity to living beauty was keen and most of these visits revolved around matters of love, so they nurtured in him this feeling in a nascent and obscure form. He looked forward to these visits and appointments, in which he found a vague but wonderful pleasure.

We must also say that he did not violate the trust of Uncle Salih or the oath he had made him take when he entrusted him with these dangerous books. He never catered to the desire of a young man to attract a veiled girl or a married woman, nor did he cater to a wife who wanted to strike her fellow wife with blindness or even just alienate their husband's love from her. He would only respond to married couples that wished to strengthen their love, or persuade a man to return to the wife he had divorced, or encourage a young man to propose to the girl who loved him. As for knowing the destinies of people, there was nothing that prevented him from revealing what the stars had in store. Such instruction was computed in his great book.

From this point of view he was well satisfied, content with his library, with his knowledge, and with his reputation among others.

But there was another book, of which there was only one copy in the entire village, owned by an older youth related to him. He wanted this book very much, for it would have completed his reputation in the village as someone of culture. But this unique book remained an object of desire that was beyond his grasp.

If there had been another copy of the book available, he would have purchased it. He would have asked Uncle Salih to procure it for him at any cost. But alas! It was a manuscript written by the Prophet Solomon (Peace be upon him), and Solomon was long dead. It seems that Solomon—may God's mercy be upon him—had written only one copy of the book, which fell into the hands of his young relative. He had received it from a Maghribi who revealed to him its secrets.[11] If only he would return!

This youth had risked life and limb and purchased the book for two whole sacks of flour, which he had pilfered from the grain storage. And that was in addition to money supplied by his mother, who welcomed this rare and valuable book. The book in question was *The Book of Treasures*. All of the money and riches on the face of the earth could not have equaled one hundredth of the treasures that were buried inside this book. But those treasures were guarded and could not be revealed except by killing the guards, which mostly were enchanted roosters or dogs, or jinn servants. These could be done away with only by means of special incense and talismans and death-defying procedures.

The Maghribis were specialists in such matters, and used to come one after another to the village. The village was filled with treasures, including one in the vicinity of the village's church and monastery. The monastery was hidden away in the hills and extended over an area some five kilometers long, all of it filled with treasures of every kind. In fact, there was a treasure even in the house of his maternal grandfather, and once they had almost got to it when the Maghribi's incense gave out. The incense always ran out before the job was completed, and it took a lot of money for him to bring more from faraway lands fraught with many dangers. If he were fortunate he would return and if he did not they would ask God to replace him and their money. In fact, it appeared that he would never return, or, that if he did come and bring some more incense, it would once again run out.

An enchanted rooster guarded the treasure in his maternal grandfather's house. The only way to get rid of it was to have the sorcerer sit in a dark corner of the room with the incense in front of him. He would place a copper cup on top of the incense and begin to cast spells. The cup would fly to the opposite corner of the room and land there. Then the earth would split open and the rooster would fly out flapping its wings and screeching. The foundations of the house would tremble violently and the house would almost collapse. At that moment a group of men, armed with rifles, would fire at the rooster, while the sorcerer continued with his incantations and incense. If they hit it, the treasure would be revealed. But if they missed, their lives would be in danger. On one occasion they managed to get through all of these steps except the last one. The men swore that they had seen the pot fly, the ground open up, and the rooster fly away. They had heard it screech and aimed their rifles at it. But then the incense went out and the place turned dark and all the men fell down in a fit. The "guard" would have killed them if the sorcerer had not uttered the Great Name of God, which was the only thing that saved them. The Maghribi left to fetch more incense. Until today they still wait for him, or for another Maghribi.

So, if our young friend had owned this book, everything in his life would have been different, but his relative was stingy with this book. It was the source of imaginary but tempting wealth. And although the wealth was not immediately available, it was nevertheless inevitable that a Maghribi would bring the needed incense from dangerous tracts and deserts. His relative continued to wait while embarking upon some procedures that he could do with his book, until he wound up in a beautiful imaginary world of his own, free of all restrictions, and there he found his treasures without incantations or talismans and without incense or a book. He now lives in this beautiful free world and fully enjoys this rich treasure.

As for our child, he came to be content with his share of books and continued to be a loyal customer to Uncle Salih. Gradually, piece by piece, his library became the source of continuous cultural activity. He collected valuable books, which were borrowed by everyone. But in the last two years of his residency in the village a momentous occurrence took place that no one expected.

It was toward the end of the First World War. The school had a
young principal enflamed with patriotism. Because the boy's father
was a committee member of the Nationalist Party and a subscriber to
a daily newspaper, his home became a meeting place for the men of
the village who were Nationalist Party supporters. Included in this
group was the young headmaster, who established a close friendship
with our friend's father. The boy was allowed to attend some of the
discussions that took place during these meetings but others took
place secretly and no one knew anything about them. He could hear
the names of "Our Effendi" 'Abbas, Shaykh 'Abd al-'Aziz Jawish,
Muhammad Farid, Anwar Pasha Turki, Tal'at and Ra'uf and his ship
the *Hamidiyya*, which caused the Allies pain and about which leg-
endary stories were told.[12]

The feelings of the entire village were on the side of Turkey, the
State of the Islamic Caliphate, and against the Allies, who represented the "unbelievers" and were fighting Islam. It seemed that certain feelings were beginning to ferment. He remembers that now and
realizes that even though he was a child he, like the men, had the
feeling that some as yet ill-defined thing was going to happen. He did
not know what it was or how it would occur, but that it would definitely happen. Secret meetings took place at his house. Doors were
shut and voices were reduced to whispers. These meetings impressed
in his mind this ill-defined thing that he did not know.

Gradually he began to get involved in what the adults were doing,
especially because he was already in his fourth year at primary school
and often took over from his father the task of reading the newspaper
to the group that assembled at their house to hear it. This, plus the
fact that he was at the top of his class, especially in the Arabic language lessons, drew him to the attention of the headmaster, who decided that he was qualified enough to be lent two great books. In
these books the boy found something quite different from anything
in his library, for all the diverse material it contained.

One of these was a collection of poetry by a man named Thabit al-Jurjawi. The other was a book of history by Muhammad Bey Khudari,[13] whose introduction contained a picture of 'Abbas II and a tribute to his achievements.

The poetry collection was made up of patriotic poems, which the boy now realizes were extremely weak and naïve verses. But at the time he regarded them as a literary marvel because they were superior to the bits of poetry he had already memorized.

> Usluk bunayya manahij al-sadat
> Wa-takhallaq anna bi-ashraf al-adat
> [Follow, my son, the paths of the noble ones,
> And embrace the most honorable customs]

Or:

> Ahsin ila al-nas taasta'bidu qulubahum
> Fa-talama ista'bada al-insana ihsan
> [Be kind to a people and you will captivate their hearts
> For, as is known, humans are captured by kindness]

Or:

> Dhu al-Asba' al-'Adwani, advising his son, said: "Acquire money and increase it. Wealth is the means for noble deeds, an aid against fate, and a force against debt. It is likewise an object of familiarity among brothers, and a helper against the twists of fortune."

Such words really meant nothing to him. They were merely words that he had memorized.

He found in this poetry words that nourished in his soul the spirit of patriotism, a spirit that had been awakened by the family atmos-

phere in which he lived and the general atmosphere that was as if
charged with electric currents ready to explode. He still recalls some
verses, such as:

> My homeland is dear, I would have no other,
> however sore beset by its foes.

> I sleep and awake, my whole being ablaze,
> its anthem proclaims its cause to the crowd.

And finally:

> Thabit al-Jurjawi has spoken in his history,
> "My homeland is dear, I would have no other!"

The value of this book increased for our friend when he learned
that its author was a political prisoner and that the administrative
laws that were in effect at that time had banned the collection.

As for the book of history, it meant a great deal to him that its author wrote at the end of its introduction, "This book will perhaps not
be printed again, unless these sections are deleted." He was referring
to the passages immortalizing the Khedive 'Abbas Hilmi II.

Thus he had in his hands two valuable and rare books containing
patriotic material of the kind that his soul thirsted for. Because he
could not imagine that there were any other books comparable to
these nor that their owner would ever give them to him, he used another way to get possession of them: He collected blank sheets of
paper from all of his notebooks from previous years, and in so doing
was able to create one large blank notebook. He already had enough
pens and ink. He then began with admirable patience and persever-
ance to copy the collection, verse by verse, into his notebook, and he
also copied the introduction to the historical work, which would not

be reprinted until the offending passages were removed. Today he marvels at how he was able to make such a great effort. But what is even more amazing is that he was able to memorize the collection by heart. He is still able to recall it after many years.

When he rushed out into the village to tell his friends what he had memorized and claimed that it was by a poet who was living at that time, no one believed him. For poetry was a feature of the early inhabitants of the Arabian Peninsula. Since that time no one was thought capable of composing a single verse of poetry. When he supported his case by pointing to other living poets of whom he learned from his great teacher, one of which was Shawqi and the other Hafiz,[14] everyone still denied his claim, which was simply unbelievable.

He desired to prove his case and so they made a wager, waiting patiently for one of the scholars who were studying in Cairo at the Azhar, or the fellow who was studying at Dar al-'Ulum,[15] or the one who was studying in the faculty of law, to come by (You can see that the village had made great progress) and decide the serious matter.* He was confident that in his own age there were men who composed poetry and prose like what he read in textbooks. He had evidence for the existence of poetry in the poetry collection and in what the teacher had told him of Shawqi and Hafiz. As for prose, his evidence was the dictation piece given to them during the exam. The teacher himself had composed it: "Regard the camel. See his long neck and rectangular head, created in such a way as to balance the body. . ." This was more elegant prose than any other! And a contemporary man had created it!

He then heard that that man who was studying at Dar al-'Ulum would come to the village during the summer holidays to deliver ser-

---

*Author's note: This has all changed. Daily newspapers, weekly and monthly magazines, and literary books have come to the village, and among its inhabitants are a number who can compose poetry and prose.

mons of his own creation, not ones derived from books. He was doubtful about this despite the fact that some of the man's relatives swore as to the veracity of this miracle, and claimed that they had seen him "create it from his mind" and not take it from a book.

When the trumpet blew for the great Egyptian revolution, the principal stood before the assembled students and delivered a fiery patriotic speech. He said that the school would be closed indefinitely because he and his colleagues were leaving to work for the revolution. It was every person's duty to do so! Then occurred the miracle that he sometimes doubted and sometimes believed in. And it came into being by his very own hands. He exploded in enthusiasm for the revolution and wrote speeches to which he added verses of poetry— he considered them well composed but in fact they were quite weak. He delivered them in meeting halls and mosques, where the spirit of the sacred revolution was breathed into all, so that they would listen to everyone who acclaimed the revolution, even if it was a small boy like him who was hardly more than ten years old.

Then came the new sacred name—the name of Sa'd Zaghlul![16]

8   The Law of the Thieves

The boy was able to overcome in his mind the myth of the *'afarit* and to walk around the twisted roads of the village feeling safe, or nearly so. But he was not able to overcome the terror that possessed him whenever he ran into that disgusting creature, the one named Harhur!

This Harhur would sit on the mud-brick bench outside his house holding in his hand his spindle or sometimes his stave and would smile at the boy whenever he passed by on the way to his grandfather's house. His wife would sit inside the open door watching the comings and goings and would peek at him and smile and invite him in. Nevertheless, he still dreaded Harhur and loathed his wife, even after he got a bit older and was able to think more calmly. This Harhur was a thief, though not the only thief in the village. Still he, more than all the others of whom the boy had heard, instilled in him this terror that rapidly changed in his soul to loathing, so that he would rather encounter the devil than this man whether by day or by night.

Harhur's wife was not originally from the village. Rather, she was a gypsy who had fallen in love with Harhur when he was young. Then he "possessed" her, as the villagers put it when talking about lovers, and then married her. She fell in love with him because he was one of those assassins called "the scions of night," as the nastiest of the

97

thieves were called. These do not refrain from murder, but rather treat it as a game they play during their numerous adventures. Then three daughters were born to him, and they grew up to be exactly like their mother. They developed a special reputation. The house and those who lived in it became a source of terror for mothers who feared for their adolescent sons and for wives whose husbands might be seduced away from them by that horrible house.

The child had a half-brother who, though a full generation older than he, was still young and had some involvement with this house. The whole family whispered to one another about that tie with terror and fear. The child heard about these matters as he was growing up, but did not know the real story. He imagined that the people in this house really kidnapped youth who were then never seen again. Because he loved his brother, he always feared for him because of that den of perdition! Then he came to understand the real story, but this knowledge simply added loathing to his original fear and terror. As a result he always avoided passing by that dreadful place, right up until the time he departed the village as a teen. Indeed, to this day he feels a certain shuddering when he passes this house!

But Harhur was not alone in the village, for thievery was for the most part a recognized profession in the countryside, a profession with its principles, its traditions, and indeed its laws known by all. Furthermore, it was a field open to youth of all social classes—including the sons of the wealthy who could not be said to steal in order to eat. It was a kind of *futuwwa*,[1] which they called "showing their prowess," that was practiced by a youth as a way of channeling the energy stored in his body, which could find no outlet except through this despicable nightly activity.

Many of these joined gangs of thieves—those good-for-nothing, thrill-seeking sons of the night. They were attracted by the adventures that they heard about, which, rather than being criticized by the public, attracted admiration instead. (This may be a remnant of a Bedouin tradition that penetrated the Egyptian environment and that considers assault and plundering to be forms of heroism and bravery.) It was characteristic of these youths that they did not take a share of the booty. They did not go out for the stealing but rather for the adventure. If the gang got something, their share of it went to the gang or to some member of it who had been prevented from participating by some serious matter, such as being in prison or having been injured in a previous venture. Thus, that person's share kept coming to his family until he could once again perform his "noble" work. That was one of the laws of the thieves. Another was "man-to-man engagement," which means that one did not rob a house that did not have a man living in it or whose men were feeble and weak. The thief who robbed the house of a widow or a weak person was considered a "stinking" thief and was despised both by his fellow thieves and by the villagers, while the great thieves who robbed the wealthy and powerful received the respect, as well as the fear, of all. Another law of the thieves was that the village should be divided into territories, each under the control of a particular gang or gang member. It was unacceptable for one gang to intrude upon the territory of another gang. If that occurred, then the insult was requited and the shame was erased by blood. Otherwise the gang or great thief would have lost his respect, not only in his own village but in the neighboring towns also.

Sometimes the thief or the gang would impose a tax on individuals in return for protection from robberies. If someone else violated anyone enjoying this protection, then he also violated the protection and its sponsors. The stolen goods had then to be returned without "ransom" or else blood would be shed to protect the sponsors' lofty honor.

This ransom was an extraordinary affair: A robbery would take

place in a house or in a field. Cattle or some equipment from an artesian well, used to irrigate the land between the floods, would be
stolen. Almost always the village 'umda knew about the theft beforehand, as was also the case with many killings. He was guaranteed a
certain portion of the things that were stolen in return for the protection that he offered the culprits, in case the police were informed.
And rare was the man who was so naïve as to inform the police and
thus lose forever what had been stolen. Rather, the usual procedure
was that when morning arrived the whole village came to know that
the house or field of so-and-so had been robbed, that it had been
robbed by a certain person from the town or by one of the many
thieves of another town, all of whom were well known. Each gang
had a "manager," an idle man who, without actually participating in
the adventure, was responsible for the distribution of what the gang
stole. For this role he was guaranteed a certain portion.

The owner of the stolen property would go to this manager and
ask him if he had it. If he did have it, he would answer "yes," safely and
confidently. But if he did not, he would tell the owner frankly that his
property was with so-and-so—another manager—or that his property had "flown the coop," that it was gone and that there was no way
to recover it. Thieves who had stolen an animal often feared that they
would be caught and so they would slaughter the animal and sell its
meat, or else sell what they had stolen to another gang far away to
dispose of it, if they realized that there was little chance to hide it
nearby. But if the manager said that he had the item or could get it,
then they would begin to bargain about the "ransom." This was the
price that the owner of the item had to pay in order to get back what
had been stolen from him. Usually the price was half its value. The
bargaining began when the manager stated the figure demanded. The
owner would then respond that the price was unfair and too harsh,
and sometimes add that he was a poor man and that his condition demanded some sympathy. Most of the time the bargaining was effec-

tive, and the "ransom" was reduced a little. If this succeeded, the item was returned with no further ado. If not, the victim would leave and send a mediator to bargain with the manager, and he was sometimes able to "shake down," or diminish the ransom. The manager's argument was always the same, that he was merely an honest broker and that the matter was not in his hands. Invariably the response to this claim was, "No, sir, you are everything and we know that!" Exchanges such as this always ended up with the price being paid, and the stolen property returned, for honor, by God, honor, served to dictate this outcome in the law of the thieves!

If the stolen property were returned after the ransom had been paid, the law of the thieves required that the returned goods be protected from further robberies. Honor demanded that the same item not be stolen twice. This protection could be either full or partial. Partial protection meant simply that the gang or the thief did not steal the returned property again. Full protection meant that the gang or the thief protected that property from further robberies by other thieves, and considered any intrusion on that property to be an affront to his own honor.

If, on the other hand, the owner of the item chose to go the legal route, he would inform the 'umda, and he in turn would not fail to inform the authorities, for he too was a man of honor, but that would be the end of things. The stolen property was lost and the owner might expect another robbery from which nobody could protect him, unless one of the inhabitants of the house happened to be awake or there was an honest watchman who feared God, and these were very few.

The invasion of homes and fields was not always for the purpose of stealing, but could occur for the purpose of revenge. The wicked man would attack the house, stab the cattle or rip its guts with a long knife that might or might not be contaminated with a poisonous substance, and all of this would be undertaken for the purpose not of stealing the cattle, but of taking revenge against their owner. He might destroy the mechanisms of the water wheel or else burn them, or the machinery of the artesian well, or the cattle trough, all for the purpose of taking revenge. In such cases it was not a matter of "ransom" but further revenge. And this is what usually happened. Either the "favor" was returned to the house of the thief and his fields and cattle—and most of the thieves had fields, cattle, and of course a house in the village—or he was ambushed and killed in one way or another. Seldom did news of such an incident reach the police authorities. This would bring the legal officer to investigate and, if necessary, a medical examiner. And the village got very nervous in the presence of officialdom. Moreover, this rarely accomplished anything, because the witnesses usually vanished either out of fear of the perpetrators or in order to let the people involved settle things among themselves without interference. They did not want to be seen as too weak to take their own revenge, and it was only the weak that have recourse to the government.

It was similar as regards vendetta killings. These incidents occurred all the time, and their fire kept burning generation after generation. Perhaps a man was killed who had one young child. The child's mother, along with the rest of the people in the village, would keep telling him the story of his father's murder until he was ready to take vengeance simply because he had the strength to do so. Only then was the funeral of the father performed and only then did his family accept condolences; otherwise, the family would continue to be shamed before the village. None of them could raise their heads before he took vengeance.

It usually happened that the 'umda was out of the village for a few days before a murder took place. People interpreted such a coincidence and concluded that there was a secret understanding. In every case the *'umda* was not held responsible for the crime or required to collect evidence because he was not present in the days immediately before and after it.

Two horrible events are inscribed in the boy's memory and imagination. The first occurred on a day when his aunt, her husband, and her children awoke to find all of their cattle either stabbed in the stomach, their guts ripped apart, or poisoned by a caustic substance that had been inserted in their stomach. That incident was particularly horrible and cruel. He saw the cows writhing from the deadly pain, though they were not guilty of anything except that a wicked man sought to take a terrible revenge on their owner.

The legal officer came, and also a veterinary doctor, as he remembers, who tried everything he could to save the life of these animals. But he failed except for one calf whose stomach he was able to cleanse of the poison. The calf survived while the others died, writhing and bellowing in pain. Tears flowed from the eyes of the humans. This time the doctor was not a source of terror and fear. Rather, the people felt that he was a messenger of mercy even to the animals.

As for the second incident, the child did not witness it himself, but he heard the story of it related dozens of times. It was the talk of the whole village. It made his body tremble. Yet he recalls that story again and again while his imagination follows its scenes in fascinated terror. The story involved three youths, one of whom had married his uncle's daughter. The uncle wanted him to divorce her, but he refused. So the uncle filed one of those malicious lawsuits against him in the family court.[2]

One day during the sessions, the young man was on his way to the court, which was in the city, with his two brothers. Green fields stretched between the village and their destination and the road that travelers followed narrowed into a thin path surrounded by high plants, so that another person could be discerned only at a short distance. The three brothers had set out very early in the morning. They had no animals to ride because they were poor and so were walking from the village to the city, a distance of some ten kilometers. They had to leave earlier than people with animals in order to arrive on time, because the court opened at sunrise. If, upon their arrival, the court was not yet open, they would sit in front of it until they were let in. Such was their awe of the court that it seemed safer to arrive hours before the session was to take place.

The shameless uncle found this out and so, along with two armed thugs whom he had hired, he set out ahead of them to lay an ambush at an isolated place along the road where they could not be seen by any riders passing by. When the brothers passed by, the thugs stabbed two of them and they fell to the ground. The third saw what was happening and fled, pursued by the three men. He screamed in terror, but there was no one in those sleepy fields to help him. Finally they caught him and took him into to a field of beanstalks that were tall as a man. There they also dragged the two wounded brothers, well away from the road, and finished them off, while the third brother watched but could not scream.

Then it was his turn. He pleaded with his monstrous uncle in a way that would have softened iron, saying to him: "Why do you want to kill me, uncle? What wrong have I done to you? Do not my brothers suffice? You have already killed your opponent so let me go. My mother is alone and I am her only support now that my brothers are gone and the only support of the small child that your brother left behind. Free me for God's sake and I will remain silent about all that has happened. I swear to you!"

But the pitiless uncle did not listen to any of that. He was afraid that if he freed him, the third brother would testify against him and his two accomplices. It is said that the third brother kept pleading for half an hour, but his uncle never softened up. In the end, the two thugs finished off the poor man.

The criminals did their deed and departed. The three corpses were left and no one knew anything about it. The day passed and the brothers did not come back to their waiting mother. Then came the morning and the evening of the second day and by then she was desperate with anxiety. On the third day the worst was suspected and rumors circulated, pointing first to one and then another but finally settling squarely in the loathsome face of that wicked uncle.

God's eye was not unmindful of the criminals and the investigation led to them. It was said that the investigator for the prosecution sometimes forgot his job and became so overwhelmed with rage that he wished that the fourth brother, who was but a lad, had impetuously attacked the monstrous uncle and killed him in his presence. Then he could have claimed in his report that the youth had done so in a state of madness, brought on by the thought of the bodies of his three brothers with their bellies torn open and their guts ripped out and then the insolent uncle right in front of him reminding him of that horrible crime! But the boy wasn't up to that, and perhaps it was only the village imagination that made people think the investigator felt that way. Or perhaps indeed the investigator's feelings were as the villagers pictured them in the face of such a savage and horrible crime. In any case, every time our young boy heard the story he wished that the fourth boy had drawn his knife and slashed open the belly of the savage uncle. Even though he knew that had not happened and never would, his imagination always completed the story with that desired end.

9   The Confiscation of Weapons

The village woke up terrified by the neighing of horses, the clatter of weapons, and the heavy steps of soldiers who were occupying the whole area, including the fields, and noisily searching everywhere. The village had never experienced a visit by soldiers in such numbers and with such tumult.

The first to discover what was happening were those whose work required them to rise at dawn and leave the village for the fields. The soldiers, who had taken over all of the approaches to the village, captured these and bound them with ropes and chains, making them prisoners so that they could not return and alert the villagers, and thus spoil the plans devised by the force that was now attacking the people while they slept. The same procedure was carried out on the watchmen stationed at the outskirts. Their hands were tied behind their backs and they were gagged so that they would not be able to talk or scream out. Then all the prisoners were taken in a cart to the residence of the *'umda*, who was abruptly awakened and held in one of the rooms of his house. Presently he was joined by the village's five elders, who were brought by the soldiers from their homes. They experienced the same fate as the watchmen. By now the whole village was awake and terrified. The neighing of horses, the clatter of arms, and the frightened whispers had penetrated every house and alley, scaring the people and filling their hearts with fear.

What was going on?

It was a campaign for the confiscation of weapons! A campaign of two hundred soldiers led by an officer who had pledged to the authorities that he would confiscate arms from all of the villages of the province. He chose this method of terror to begin his work, and the village did not know what he wanted, not even the *'umda* and the elders, until dozens had been arrested. All had their hands bound with rope and were slapped and kicked without gaining any idea of what was really wanted of them, except that the government was there. The government can do all this and more. Some of those who had lived during the Turkish rule were still alive.

Previously when the authorities had issued a military order to confiscate weapons, they had assigned its implementation to the men of the administration. These, as was usual, in turn delegated the *'umad* to carry it out. As a result, the same number of weapons had been collected as was collected every time an order of this kind was issued, that is, usually only a small proportion of what was actually present in the hands of the villagers.

In order to appreciate the real situation we have to understand that two groups owned the weapons in the village. The first group consisted of those who owned land and cattle. They had special guards who would spend the night protecting their property against thieves. The second group consisted of those same thieves, who were many and who found that profession—in spite of its dangers—a more assured way of making a living than tiring work in the fields. A shortage of weapons on the part of the owners of land and cattle would mean an increase in crime and in attacks on their homes, fields, and livestock. But a shortage of weapons in the hands of thieves would deprive these of some of their chosen methods of gaining their livelihood. Both sides were thus eager to acquire weapons. Because the 'umda sometimes feared members of the second group, and sometimes found their presence to be in his personal interest, the confiscation of arms was inevitably carried out at the expense of the first group.

But the affairs of the village could not be forced, nor would they proceed according to official orders. Rather, things progressed in accordance with recognized customs. Thus the 'umda knew exactly how many weapons were in each house, and of what kind. When the government demanded that weapons be confiscated, he would make an agreement with some of the owners according to which they would submit only the old pieces. And in order that the matter would not be too obvious, some new pieces would be added to adorn the collection, and it would be submitted to the authorities as representing everything that the village 'umda could get. Naturally, none of this was done for free, for everything has a price and in the countryside every service is reciprocated. Now, if it occurred to the authorities to send a force led by an officer to do the job, then the 'umda would take charge. Everything would be taken care of at his direction. A fancy lunch involving geese, cocks, chickens, and pigeon would be sufficient, along with other incentives, to settle everything and complete the proceedings to everyone's satisfaction.

But now a novel way had been devised by that genius of an officer who had pledged to the authorities to make a real collection of weapons from all of the province's villages. And so he took the brilliant and unexpected approach that, under the cover of darkness, stunned the entire village.

We return to those five elders whose hands were tied behind their backs and whose faces were stuck against the wall, with no idea as to what tasks the government would demand of them. They were accustomed to occasional demands, such as corvée labor to repair bridges and clear vermin from large fields, or to kill locusts, without getting paid for these things, because their wage—if there was any—went into other pockets. They would be fingerprinted on papers whose purpose eluded them. Then they would leave, considering themselves fortunate that they were only asked to bring their food with them from their homes throughout the period of corvée, which might vary in length.

This time, nobody explained to them what was required of them, but the soldiers' whips that burned their backs explained to them that this day was not like other days. Held captive, they were powerless to stop the painful treatment. Then bullets began to resound above their heads and above those of the trusted guards and the people who had been caught by chance at the village's outskirts and in its streets and who filled the courtyard of the residence.

These bullets were meant to terrorize, confuse, and unnerve. While this great terror overwhelmed them, unhinging their minds, each of the elders was ordered to dictate to the officer the names of two hundred heads of families who owned farms in the countryside, and to specify the types of weapons they owned.

If mind or memory remained in any one of them, they began to dictate names. Whenever one of them paused to remember, he was whipped, causing him to speed up the count and dictate names like a madman. The operation ended, and in the hand of each officer was a report of two hundred families possessing arms and before each name was the type of weapon owned by each family head.

We need not tell you what these reports were like or how closely they corresponded to reality. The elder was being crucified, whipped and threatened with death by the bullets flying above his head. In that state one could hardly expect him to give careful thought to what he said, but we can assert that not one of the names of the feared big criminals appeared on that list. If some names were listed, they were the names of the small culprits who had no support and no influence.

That stage was completed, and the five elders stood up gasping from exhaustion, fear, and pain. But the *'umda* had purchased his safety and honor from the beginning. He had been shrewd enough to see the danger coming and had moved quickly to find a means sure to appease the authorities, something he knew how to do from his long experience, practical intelligence, and general knowledge of how to get things done.

Then the next stage began. Their hands bound, the watchmen departed with the soldiers, searching with them through the village to show them the houses and knock on the doors, asking for the heads of families and insisting that the oldest ones come. As soon as they had gathered a group of these they brought them to the *'umda*'s residence. Here they were treated just as the elders and watchmen had previously been treated before being asked anything or being given a chance to respond. Only after they were sufficiently beaten, terrorized, and humiliated were they confronted with the demands for the weapons indicated in the reports. If it happened that the pieces required of an individual matched what he actually had, he felt relieved and immediately confessed, and asked permission to bring them. But his request was not granted. Rather, one of his sons or another member of his family was summoned to see him in that condition, and then himself receive some slaps and punches. Then the son or family member was ordered to bring the required pieces and ran off to get them. When they were examined and seen to match the written reports, the man and his son or relative were released, completely groggy due to the severity of the slaps and punches they had received, and the fear and terror they had experienced. His family then had to devote itself to treating his wounds with ointments and painkillers.

But if it happened that there was a discrepancy between the reports and the weapons he actually had, or if he had no weapons at all, then woe betide him. He would be whipped, slapped, and punched again and again as long as he either denied having any weapons or confessed to a weapon other than the one demanded. In the latter case, the weapon that he owned would be brought, and then they would continue to demand the other weapons that the elder had reported, while he was dazed by terror and pain! At that point the poor man would be driven to confessing to what he did not have, and would ask for time to procure the item from a distant hiding place. Meanwhile, his sons and relatives would search for a weapon that matched the reports and buy it, wherever it might be. If they did not find a weapon in the village they would mount the fastest of their animals to search for it in the surrounding villages. The guards would allow them to leave under the pretext that they were doing so to procure a weapon that they had left with a relative in those towns, knowing that the head of the family was a hostage in the hands of the authorities and that he would suffer as long as they were away. When they finally found the required weapon, they would pay whatever price the owner demanded. Many people took advantage of this opportunity and charged excessively for the required weapon. But many others also demonstrated their generosity by asking the lowest possible prices in order to deliver those in distress.

At that point, the "brilliant" officer smiled while he watched the weapons demanded being presented after having been denied, and attributed that to his unique genius that led him to take the best approach. At the end of the day the arms collected were put into piles according to type. One pile had guns, and others had handguns, revolvers, pistols, swords, large knives, axes, and spears. Within these types each model was placed separately. The great officer surveyed the scene contentedly, puffed up like a rooster at his decisive victory over the "accursed villagers."

Every house in the village was in silent mourning. This person's head was cut open, that one's ribs were bruised, another's skin was red with welts, and still another's jaw was smashed. The women and chil-

dren scurried back and forth carrying oils and cold and hot com-
presses to aid the injured. Many villagers had sold their cattle, their
children's food, and their wives' jewelry in order to buy the weapons
that were said to be in their possession, even though they had never
carried a weapon in their entire lives. These were the poor, whom
the elders used to complete the count, knowing that they were safe
from retribution because the poor had no power like the wicked
scoundrels and had no influence like the wealthy.

More than a quarter of a century has passed since that incident.
But the child still remembers it as if it happened yesterday. Like every
child, man, and woman, he had been terrified. During those years, he
heard that this monstrous officer had been promoted and, at one
point, became director of public security in acknowledgment of his
competence in maintaining security and preserving order. Consequently, the boy harbored within him a hidden feeling of despair.
Then, after that, he heard that the officer had been killed while carrying out another of his atrocious deeds. As a result, he felt that a
heavy weight had been lifted off his chest and he breathed a deep
sigh of relief.

10 The Harvest

During three seasons in the year the face of the village changed, and it came alive as if with a new soul and new feeling, especially the village children, who looked forward to these seasons from year to year. These seasons were the "wet planting" season, the harvest season, and the cotton-picking season.

Everyone knows about the second and third seasons, but the only ones who know about the first are those who live in the irrigated lands of the floodplain that are exposed for most of the year until the inundation comes in September and October, flooding the farmland so that it becomes a lake a meter deep, or in some places two or more meters deep. Then the village is transformed into a group of islands interconnected only by small boats and light skiffs. This is just as 'Amr Ibn al-'As says in a letter,[1] which the boy had memorized in primary school and whose confirmation he saw with his own eyes each year. The truth is that the vista of the expanse of water from one side of the valley to the other was unique and magical. The whole valley turned into a vast lake as the Nile had escaped from its fetters and overflowed the barrier of its banks in order to embrace its beloved earth, which it visited only once a year. And when the time came for the flood to depart, retreating a bit each day, people looked upon the Nile as if it were someone they were regretfully taking leave of. The child even heard one of the simple villagers say as he sorrowfully con-

113

templated the falling Nile, its high waves having subsided, seeping away, spent and exhausted, "poor fellow, he is done for." The man said this as if he were speaking of a living person with whom he had close ties, family links, and personal affection.

One fine day the village would wake up to find that the lake had completely retreated, that the black earth was exposed and that upon it lay that layer of silt that produced the wealth of vast stretches of the valley. The earth now sought the seed so that it might grow the coming year's food for man and beast. Then the people went out, planting their feet in the mud, sowing the seed that they carried on their shoulders, and then covering it with a layer of mud that they had cleared away using a shovel called a *lawb*. This operation was called the "wet planting," one of the three seasons known to the villages of the floodplain.

The amount of farmland held by the village was greater than the number of hands available to work it, because it was a rich village by comparison with the neighboring ones. Large quasi-feudal landholdings were not known there. The largest agricultural holding was not more than two hundred *feddans*, and there was hardly an individual or family that did not have a piece of land, whether large or small. This distribution of land diminished the class differences and created a condition of personal pride in the relationships between people. Thus there were no servants, at least in the sense that term is understood in the city and on some country estates where the status of a servant is virtually as low as that of a slave. The typical servant in this village was a poor person in need of work. He never uttered the hated phrase "my master," but replaced it with "my uncle" for the head of the household and "wife of my uncle" for his wife. Every family owned a house, whether large or small. Mud huts were not known in this village. More than half of the houses were built of brick and the rest of adobe. The majority consisted of two or three floors and some even had four. Even among the houses of the poor it was rare to find a dwelling with only one floor.

As a result of the fairly good distribution of farmland, the standard of living was reasonable by comparison with many other areas and even the poorest family had meat every week, or at least every other week. Those who could not afford meat bought such parts as tripe, shanks, heads, hearts, livers, and the like. These were very cheap compared to regular meat. Likewise clarified butter was found in all of the houses. Some mixed it with oil from animal fat and the very few Christians in the village mixed it with vegetable oil, but it was used in general with the food. And fruits and vegetables such as watermelon, cantaloupe, pomegranate, lotus fruit, cucumber, guava, country apples, and sugarcane all entered the houses in varying quantities.

Thus the village was known for its wealth, as it was for its progressiveness by comparison with the neighboring villages, especially as regards the construction of its houses and the cleanliness of its inhabitants. Admittedly this cleanliness appeared to be distressing filth when viewed with the eye of the city dweller, but everything in this life is relative.

Therefore the hands available for work did not suffice, especially in these three seasons, and so groups of "foreigners" would come every year to work in the fields. They would come from remote and rude places, from Qena and Aswan, from the desolate villages of these two provinces, where the valley narrows and the mountains press in on it violently and harshly, and where a few individuals have taken exclusive possession of the lands and hold estates, leaving the rest in want, desolation, and misery!

These "foreigners" were the ones who taught the village and its people the value of their wealth and the degree of blessing that God had showered upon them. They were "foreigners" not because they lived so far away but because of their physical appearance, which differed from that of the villagers; their clothing, if one could properly call it clothing; their obviously distorted way of speaking; and their songs, which emphasized sorrow and distress; and by all the circumstances of their lives, which turned them in the view of the villagers into "foreigners," related to them in no way except religion. So far as ethnicity was concerned, the gap was wide. They were like two different races!

They came in groups. Each group was called a *kalla* and was headed by a *rayyis,* or "boss," who recruited them, agreed on their salary, and supervised their work. In compensation for this he received a salary like one of them but without doing the same work they did.

Among these our child had gotten to know one *kalla* and one *rayyis* in particular. This was the *kalla* that had been coming to their house every season, and it varied in number between ten and fifteen men. This was the main *kalla* upon which his father relied in his farming. During busy times additional *kallas* would be contracted for a few days but after that, this particular *kallas* would stay on for the rest of the season—it was the *kalla* of the family and strong ties had developed between them. They were satisfied with each other and they had entered into something like a family relationship.

The songs of these people were plaintive ones that mixed bitterness and grief with manliness and chivalry. They roused the soul and feelings of the small boy, and he listened to them spellbound as they stirred up in his small soul emotions he did not know and could not express. But he always yearned for these men and looked forward to their return from year to year. He would ask them to keep on singing more and more when the group quieted down due to the tiredness that resulted from their burdens. And they would always respond to his request, because he was the young son of the master of the house. But he was also the friend of each one of them and particularly of the *rayyis.* All the requests they wanted to make of the household went through him and he would insist that each of their requests be attended to and would argue on their behalf if anyone objected. He would feel the greatest satisfaction when he brought them what they had requested. The world could hardly contain the joy he felt in serving the needs of his great friends.

After he went to school and solved the mysteries of handwriting, he also became their personal secretary. He could then write letters for them to their distant hometown and read them the letters that came back, which told of their children and their families. The fact that they revealed to him all of their secrets, as simple and limited as these were, spawned a new kind of friendship. He was the trusted guardian of these secrets, which he came to know from their letters that went back and forth. Perhaps they trusted his child's innocence when they entrusted these secrets to him.

Ten, twelve, or fifteen of them would write one letter together, sending it to Shaykh Muhammad Abu 'Ulaym, *shaykh* of the village of al-Kalah al-Gharbiyya and also its *ma'zun*, or notary public. All their names sounded strange to the boy's ears, but this was not surprising because they were "foreigners" and everything connected with them was strange. They would collect together all the money they wanted to send and have the boy write out a statement that gave the name of each individual and, in front of it, the amount he wanted to send. He would then take the entire amount and buy for them a postal money order in the name of Shaykh Muhammad. At their dictation he would then write to them how the amounts indicated in the statement were to be distributed to their families there.

So far as he can remember the amount accumulated was never more than two pounds. One of them would send to his family by post eight or ten piastres or at the most twenty, his face beaming and his features radiant with joy, feeling that he had sent to those he had left behind something that would take care of their needs, relieve their problems, and keep life going! Once, it occurred to him to inquire: Is that all? What will these few piastres do? He received as a response from these people a smile that lent dignity to their miserable condition and contained a simple innocent cheerfulness. Then one or more answered him in their particular Upper Egyptian accent:

"Yes, what do you say, my little man? Do you think that everyone is like you and your comfortable dad?" By this they meant "your wealthy father," because they associated wealth with comfort, and that is quite a precise way of putting it. But there was not even a glimmer of envy in their eyes or voices, nor of resentment, at these appalling differences of which they spoke in their simple words.

The system of work and payment in the village was as follows: The worker's daily wage varied from two to two and one-half piastres, in accordance with the price levels and in accordance with the need for workers and the number available, that is, in accordance with the law of supply and demand. But this wage was in addition to lodging and food, especially the evening meal. The people of the house always provided food to the workers in the evening, and sometimes for other meals. The evening meal usually consisted of meat soup and meat. The former was made of clear broth or from broth enriched with ripe onions and *kishk* with bread, and this was rich, nourishing, and tasty food. The degree of richness varied from house to house, depending on the generosity or stinginess of their hospitality, for the village generally treated them like foreign guests. Some houses provided their "foreigners" with breakfast, especially in the season of "wet planting," because they were working in the mud, where their legs would sink in up to the knees and where the "foreigner" would for the entire day carry two kilos of seed on his shoulder and still have to clear away the mud with the *lawh* and then cover the seed. Work of this kind is difficult without nourishing food. This breakfast usually consisted of wheat bread with dates and onions, or of special pastries called *mukhammar*, made with wheat flour, clarified butter, milk after letting the dough rise, and this was in addition to the bread and dates.

This was found only in the generous houses. Our child would make it a point to wake up early in the morning to bring the foreigners the largest amount of this *mukhammar* that he could stuff into the folds of his garment and his pockets, over and above their regular portion, and take it to them. Lunch usually had to be provided by the workers themselves. This normally consisted of their coarse dry bread, which they had carried with them all the way from their home villages in army sacks or in their old *gallabiyyas,* whose sleeves were tied up to become pouches for provisions and personal effects. Seldom did they contain anything more than coarse dry bread, or bread they bought in the village along with onions and salt, or salt alone most of the time.

Where could they get bread in the village? Selling bread was considered unacceptable. Indeed, it was considered the greatest shame. Each family had its house and each house had its own country-style oven. The family bought the grain, usually maize, and sieved it, cleaned it, and ground it. They used small hand sieves, and the women of the house got together with neighbors who came to help them. One group would set to sieving until the grain was cleansed of the worst of the dirt and foreign matter, and the other groups would set to sorting, that is, cleaning the grain of the fine dirt and other matter that had gotten through the sieve. That was a great day in the life of the family. Everyone in the house worked at it as well as neighbors who helped. Then it was ground and from this flour was made the bread, adding to it a bit of flour of fenugreek to hold it together and give it its special taste, which people like. So there was no need for a bread market, because only foreigners would buy bread! And even these would be given it if they asked for it from the houses, for there was no greater shame than buying and selling bread as they did in the nearby provincial capital, whose lifestyle was considered scandalous because bread was sold to people there.

But if the bread was not sold in the market, it was a recognized currency in this market! The currency in the village was comprised of banknotes or paper money, or silver or copper coins, but there were other kinds of currency, first and foremost *battau*. This was bread of pure maize or maize mixed with wheat, distinguishing it from pure wheat bread, called *raghif*, which was sometimes made the same shape as *battau*. Although the children in poor homes and in some of the middle-level ones did not generally receive daily allowances, it does not mean that they did not have anything to spend. For this, *battau* was recognized as small change in the market. The child would take some and go off to the little market and buy several handfuls of dates, and also pomegranates and a quantity of lotus fruit or a segment of sugarcane stalk, or whatever else he wished of this sort. He would also go off to the seller of *lupine* and *balila*, that is, wheat soaked in water and salt. The *battau* was in all these places the basic currency. Its value varied with the rise and fall of the price of grain generally, with its size and the mixture of ingredients, and also with how well made it was. Also, the *battau* of certain houses had a special reputation in all this, just as the currency of some countries is recognized as sound! Thus it would be recognized and valued in the market and sellers would vie for the business of those who had it and offer them tempting deals at good prices.

Battau was not the only supplementary currency in the village market, for there were other kinds of unofficial currency. These were farm produce, bran, and the droppings and excrement of chickens and pigeons. For a pocketful, capful, or pot full of these, one could buy given amounts of fruit, onions, radishes, and everything else that was for sale in the little market or the shops.

The children were not the only ones to make use of this currency. Adults did too. In fact, in comparison to the dominant currencies in the village, coins were merely supplementary, especially for small purchases. Using this bread, which accumulated from the shopkeepers, the "foreigners" bought food if they wanted to. If they had asked the townspeople for bread they would have been given it, as we have already said. But that would be begging and they were not beggars. They were proud and noble people.

Then happened the event that our boy will never forget as long as he lives. His household used to give food to the *kalla*. His mother would prepare it herself with her own hands, just as she did the family's food, seeking her reward from God for this, while his father would personally supervise the purchase of their meat from the butcher shop. He would buy the same kind of meat as he chose for the family, because otherwise the butchers would take the opportunity to slaughter skinny and old animals and lower the price a little. Many who wanted to save would accept this, and the foreigners would not find fault with any kind of meat. And generous portions of food were given to this *kalla*, bread, meat, and things to go with them.

Therefore his father was surprised when the chief of the *kalla* came and asked that they be permitted to get their food themselves in the evening, in return for an increase of a half-piastre in their wage in place of dinner.

A half-piastre? Was all this food worth only a half-piastre in their view? He was angry because they did not appreciate the hospitality he offered them. But the chief of the *kalla* hastened to disabuse him of this idea and explained to him that money was more useful to them and their families. As for food, any kind fills the stomach.

It seemed that his father was still angry, but he stopped arguing and accepted the offer and said no more. They spent four days eating outside the house and then coming back to sleep without anyone in the house having any idea how they were managing. On the fifth day they had gone out very early to finish their work in one of the fields, so that they could begin in a new field the next morning.

On that day the chief of the *kalla* asked the family through their friend, the boy, to lend them a copper cooking pot or *halla*, and the request was granted. Then they asked to use the stove on the lower floor of the house, and permission was given. (This stove consisted of two rows of adobe bricks closed off on one side with a third row, and left open on the other side. The pot was placed over the three legs and the fuel was pushed in through the open side and the fire was lit until the food cooked or the water got hot. Charcoal was rarely used and there were few kerosene stoves in the village. Also, it was believed that food cooked slowly over dung or cornstalks or cotton stalks was better than food cooked quickly over a kerosene stove.) They lit the fire and put water in the pot because they wanted to cook. Then they asked for some dry *mulukhiyya* and a bit of salt, and these were given to them. The family did not doubt that the group had bought a quantity of meat and cooking oil and a bit of onion or garlic. Otherwise, they would have asked to borrow the oil, onion, and garlic.

But what happened?

The water was boiling and they threw the salt and the *mulukhiyya* into it. Then one of them brought a stalk of dry maize and stripped it of its bark and stirred the food with it for a little while and then took it off the fire. Then they all rushed to scoop from the large copper pot with small clay pans called *maqallaya* and some of them drank the *mulukhiyya* voraciously while others finished off their pans and then crumbled their coarse dry bread into it and ate it greedily with their hands. The boy could not believe his eyes. He had been there for the whole operation, but he still could not believe it. Food without meat or oil or garlic or onions or even pepper? Could people even eat it, much less relish it as they did?

He flew upstairs to the second floor where his father, mother, and two sisters were and told them what had happened as if he were telling a fairy tale not meant to be believed, and in fact they took it that way. None of them doubted that he was playing a big joke. But he swore he was telling the truth, and their confusion increased between the tall tale on the one hand and his repeated and insistent oaths on the other. Then they went back over it with him. Perhaps he had not seen the meat and the clarified butter. Perhaps the group made their food in a way different from that of the family and he had not noticed just what they threw into their pot. He was sure, however, that his eyes had not deceived him. He asked his father to come with him so that he could ask them in his presence and thus ascertain the truth of the matter. Although his father was very proper and dignified, the very strangeness of the matter made him lose some of his gravity, and so there he was following the little child who went ahead of him as they hastily descended the stairs to find out about this serious matter.

His father learned that what his son had said was true. He was rubbing his hands with amazement and bewilderment at what these people were doing, and he announced that from the following day they would eat their usual food in the house while still getting the half-piastre they had asked for. Their tongues all burst out in prayer to God and the palms of their hands turned upward in praise on account of this great and generous man. The father went away before the group finished praying for his happiness and long life and health for his children. The boy, however, did not go away, for he was troubled about his friends and had a strong desire to know more about their real lives, especially as he had suppressed his curiosity when they sent him on small errands. He had asked only one question and had received the same answer each time, so he had stopped asking this question.

He had learned many things this night. He had learned that in the life of the people meat is a rare treat, which they taste only yearly on 'Eid al-Adha.[2] He had learned that clarified butter is something unknown in their world, because vegetable oil—especially the cheap oil that is reasonably plentiful in their lives—is sufficient for food without clarified butter. He learned that wheat is a substance with which they have no connection, but that maize is sufficient, if God takes pity on them and supplies them with the coarse maize bread that they now carry. He learned that sugar is a substance that they know of as something found in the houses of the rich, such as Shaykh Muhammad Abu 'Ulaym, the one to whom they entrust their money and their families while they are away. His wealth and God's blessings on him have reached the point that he may use up a "loaf" of sugar every month for his household and in the coffee for the many guests who come to his house. He learned that these few piastres that they sent to their families five or six times a year represented their family income for the whole year, for which they waited impatiently, except for those who "made the voyage," that is, who went to Cairo or other places to get "city work," and these provided more because one of them might send one or two pounds to his family in the course of the year.

He learned many things, whose profound effects on his soul and whose harsh impact on his feelings have only become evident as he now reflects on them from time to time, and feels shame in the depth of his soul and contempt for himself and his people. He is a robber. He has robbed these "foreigners" and many millions like them who create the wealth of the Nile Valley yet go hungry. He is a robber! If there were a just law in the valley, it would send him to prison before those multitudes whom the law counts as robbers and criminals. This was the feeling that always kept coming over him whenever he sat down to eat rich food or sweet fruit or luxurious sweets or whenever he enjoyed the simple pleasures of life amidst the millions of deprived.

11   Sorrows of the Countryside

The child's small heart knew the bitterness of sorrow too soon. It was that day when he returned from school and entered the house as usual and there was his mother lamenting, grieving audibly, repeating in a soft voice one of those many poetic phrases that are used when lamenting, and tears were flowing copiously from her eyes. She tried to fight them back when she saw him, but could not. He was no more than ten years old and this was the first time he had seen her crying. He had seen her dejected before, but as soon as he would ask her, "What is wrong, mother?" she would put on a smile and answer, while clasping him to her breast, "Nothing! Nothing! Just a bit tired."

But this time she was crying openly. The tears cascaded from her eyes, and now she was not putting on a smile or hiding her pain. Here he was, standing perplexed a few steps away from her, as if he sensed something evil and so did not utter a word but stood silently before her. She noticed him there staring at her and tried to fight back her flowing tears but could not. Then she pulled herself together and called him to her, and he threw himself into her lap and buried his face in her breast. The blackness of her grief had communicated itself to his small heart, and here he was crying without knowing the cause of his crying or of hers.

At this point the mother's heart was aroused, as was her anxiety for her only son. At that time he was still her only son, having a sister who was three years older and another three years younger. She had not yet been granted his younger brother or his two younger sisters, as a result of which their family's continued existence would be assured. Now she was caressing him and hugging him to her with tenderness while he was lost in his tears. When she asked him to calm down, he asked her not to cry again. She said if he could calm his fears perhaps she could calm hers.

"I will not cry, my son, as long as you live. The *baraka* is in you. And, I swear by your lives"—she meant him and his two sisters—"you children and your father are sufficient for me."

The boy became quiet. He looked at his mother's face and saw that her tears had dried and that she was really active and cheerful. Her cheerfulness infected him and gave him the courage to ask her, "What is wrong, mother?"

She looked him in the eyes. It seemed as if she felt that her child had become a man and that the time had come to acquaint him with some of her worries, so she said to him:

"If I speak to you, sir, do you promise me that you will be a man?"

This word "man" jolted him, for he wanted very much to grow up quickly, and he said:

"Most certainly."

She said, "Today your father sold a piece of land."

Up to that time he had not really known the meaning of this. He had been sent to school when young and had been immersed in school life. He had not concerned himself with the conditions of agriculture or the *fellahin* as had others of his age in the village, who would have understood the meaning of that sentence if it had been uttered to one of them.

As he seemed somewhat puzzled about the meaning of this information and its connection with his mother's crying, she added:

"This means that our land is decreasing and, in fact, has decreased a number of times before by such sales, for your father sells a portion of our soil from one year to another, and if things continue this way the day will come when we will have no land, no fields, and no house, no animals, and nothing of all that you see now."

Now he had understood—or sensed—the magnitude of the catastrophe that threatened him, threatened him personally. Would he lose this "field" where he used to go on Fridays to run and jump merrily and play with the people who worked there and with those who took care of their animals? Their animals! Would he lose these animals? And especially, would he lose the cow that he cherished, which they kept even while they changed the other animals, because she had the special quality of providing milk and cream in abundance? More important than that was the firm friendship that bound him to her as it also did his sisters and his mother. She had been there almost the whole time he and his sisters were growing up and had become a "personality" dear to him and to all in the house.

And the house . . . would he lose this house? At this point he felt for it affection such as he had never felt before. Their spacious, beautiful house. And the well that belonged to it, that well from which their animals and all the animals of the street drank. He took pride in this well because it was on their property and was needed by the people. These people complimented them when they brought their animals to its trough and flattered him in particular when he looked them and their animals over. He felt greatly elated that their house had this great and unique distinction, namely, that their cows and their other animals did not have to leave their property to drink as other people's animals did.

Then the "oven porch," that room specifically set aside for the second floor oven, to be distinguished from the oven on the first floor—and this was another special advantage, because other people had only one oven due to the limited space in their houses. Their house, however, which they were threatened with losing, had two ovens, one used in the winter for warmth, located on the first floor, and the other used only for bread in the summer. The latter was in a room whose ceiling had an opening to let the smoke out and whose wall was partly cut away for the same purpose. This allowed him and his older sister to jump off and back onto the wall where it was cut away while their younger sister tried but could not. So they would tease her a bit while she cried and then they would take hold of her together and pass her up and down between them.

Then there was the *makhash*, a very long, unroofed space along the side of the house where they stored the straw and the stalks of dry maize and the cotton stalks, so as to avoid the danger of fire that resulted from using the roof for storage as was the custom in the village. Their property was large enough to give their house this other special advantage, this *makhash* in which the piled straw brought one closer to the first floor roof terrace. This enabled him and his older sister easily to jump from the roof of the first floor onto the straw without danger and then race each other back up the ladder to the roof to jump again. Then there was the private alley in front of the house, which was his playground where he and his young playmates would play ball and the various simple village games.

Dozens of these beloved images passed through his mind in a fleeting instant. He wished he could put his hands around each one of these images and hold onto it for fear that it would slip away. Were they really in danger of losing all of this? He did not believe anything that had been said, and he turned toward his mother as if angry and said:"But why is my father selling this land?"

She said: "Because he owes money to people and has to repay it."

But that answer was not adequate, for why did he owe people money? How could that be when the boy always saw plenty of money in his father's long white purse, with which he bought everything?

Perhaps she realized at that moment that she had made a mistake and told the small child these things too soon, so she tried to end the discussion and distract him from it, but he insisted on knowing. So she gave him a full explanation, which allowed him to understand that his father spent more each year than he took in and had to make up the difference by selling some of the land. Now he understood the whole situation and sensed the true nature of the danger, but it was more than his small mind could do to imagine the final outcome of things, so he said: "No, mother. We will not sell our house and our field, or these animals of ours. And we will not sell our old cow!" His mother seemed to relax and take hope in these simple words of her child. She said: "May God listen to you, my son."

Then she clasped him to her, then pushed him away a bit and looked into his eyes. Concentrating in the tone of her voice all the warmth of her faith, she said: "Listen, sir, you must get back what your father has lost!"

Although the warmth of her conviction penetrated to his heart, standing there in her presence he still could not understand how he could undertake such a marvelous task, and he looked at her seeking an explanation!

She said: "When you get older you will go to Cairo and stay with your uncle and you will get an education there and become an *effendi* and receive a salary. Then you will remember that our lands in the village were sold because your father spent too much and you will be careful with your money. Likewise, you will not waste it like your older brother but will spend only what is necessary. Then you will have lots of money in your pocket and you will buy back these lands that we have lost."

And while she was going on and on about her sweet dreams, which she expected her small child to fulfill, his imagination was dwelling on the trip to Cairo and on the *effendi* that he would be, and he did not pay attention to the rest of what she said.

He snapped back to attention, however, and was dumbfounded as she continued: "You must not be a spendthrift like your uncles, for they are like your father in their spending, perhaps even worse. Let me tell you that they sold their vast lands and all their many houses except for one small one."

Now he paid attention because he was already aware of these painful facts. He had not witnessed the beginning of the tragedy, but he was well aware of it as he went about the village and heard it from the mouths of the women and some of the men, just as he heard his mother recount it bitterly again and again. His grandfather on his mother's side had been very wealthy, but as soon as his four uncles grew up, two of them going to the Azhar and two of them remaining as farmers, they all became extremely extravagant. As soon as his grandfather died they squandered the wealth left and right until it was all gone. It turned out that the best-off of them was this uncle who worked as a teacher and a journalist in Cairo. With him lived the boy's grandmother, whom he loved almost to the point of worship and whom he saw on rare occasions. When his mother depicted the fate that awaited his father's house if things continued as they were going, he could see the yawning abyss. Thus the first seed of real responsibility was sown in his soul. He knew now why his mother was pushing his education so fast and why she had been so eager for him to go to the primary school rather than the *kuttab*. He had to repair the building before it collapsed.

Many women in the village bore the same worries and fears that his mother did, but did not have the hope she had in her young children, because they did not have a brother in Cairo. Cairo, in the minds of the villagers, was always associated with great happiness and a radical change of condition. That was because for many middle-class families in the village wealth was limited, because it was divided up by inheritance generation after generation, and by the third or fourth generation had almost dwindled away, unless there was an unexpected change of fortune. A good family could find itself in financial straits, and sometimes miserable poverty, while dwellings once inhabited and full of life could become melancholy ruins. The memory of these things would persist in the soul of each individual and particularly among the women, and so grief would dominate the house and gloom close it off, unless a new hope dawned.

The sorrows of the countryside are long and drawn out because time there moves with slow and plodding steps. Death, which assails one member of the family after another, always casts a thick black shadow, perching on every breast and appearing in every gesture. The country people hold onto their sorrows for a long time, finding in them nourishment for their souls, which are overshadowed by miseries on all sides: There are the bitter miseries of poverty following wealth, the painful miseries of poverty inherited from previous generations, and the miseries of death and its ceremonies. The death rate in the countryside is high, as is the birthrate, which compensates for it. But each death is a lasting memory in the heart of the mother or spouse or sister, which continues to exude grief whenever it is triggered by a funeral or some incident. She then takes refuge in sorrowful and melancholy lamentation.

When the men are in the fields they can forget. The bright sunlight fills their souls and brightens them, and the sprouting of the seeds in the black earth causes dim hopes to grow in their souls even though in their profound simplicity they cannot fully perceive them. But the women, who generally do not leave the houses—except for the very poor who on rare occasions go into the field in the Upper Egypt—these women have nothing to make them forget their sorrows. The houses are dark and their rooms are gloomy, especially when night falls and the houses are lit only by those dim, small kerosene lamps, which give forth their weak, pale light onto the dark walls, so that people's shadows dance upon them like specters, and a gloomy feeling of distress and sorrow settles over the house and those in it.

Then there is the dark-colored clothing. Only a bride in the early years of her marriage is allowed in this environment to adorn herself and wear beautiful clothes and to act lightheartedly. When the years pass and she gets older and reaches thirty, she must behave "modestly." If she continues with her adornment and beautiful clothes and her gaiety, tongues wag about her behavior and she becomes the object of criticism from all sides, and this at the age when her city cousin is just beginning to really enjoy life.

The economic factor enters into all of this, for it costs money to have beautiful clothes and to keep them clean all of the time, but dark clothes wear well and do not show the dirt, and so are more economical. The people, however, do not like to admit that it is economic considerations that determine their behavior, so they turn it into an ethical matter. The girl or woman who does not adorn herself and does not keep her clothes clean is the desired ethical model!

There is one month in the year when the village rejoices and forgets its sorrows, and that is the month of Ramadan. The secret of this rejoicing is, in the first place, the light—the light that shines from the many houses that are hosting parties at night, where doors are opened to visitors and the Qur'an is recited throughout the month. Then there are the lamps that hang from some of the doors to guide the many passersby who stay out late at night because they feel safe from the *'afarit*, which are fettered during the month of Ramadan in accordance with their ancient pact with the prophet Solomon.

The rejoicing is not only because of the light, however, but also because of the food. The whole town, both rich and poor, prepares for this blessed month with special and excellent food, both for *iftar* and *suhur*. People cook almost every day and they eat meat and fruit in ample quantities, and there is plenty of activity in preparing for all of this. So when the village finds light and food during the month of Ramadan, it buries and forgets its sorrows and rejoices in life, free from deprivation and gloom.

This phenomenon is repeated during other festivals and special occasions, especially the *mawlid* of the Prophet, because of the abundance of the two basic ingredients of happiness. Then the unaccustomed activity dies down and the town returns to its dark gloom, to its inherited deprivation and its traditional sorrows, for it likes to dwell on these sorrows, which it calls "the burdens of fortune."

Among the "the burdens of fortune" may be listed the burden of poverty, the burden of deprivation, and the burden of the rulers' injustice. For the countryman is always oppressed by the rulers, oppressed by the taxes on his small bit of earth, oppressed by the endless demands of the *'umda* to meet the orders of the government, which include donations for charitable associations collected from the neediest people, the ones who should be receiving assistance from the charitable associations, tickets for the Red Crescent, tickets for the first aid service. Then there is the corveé labor on the dikes and in the fields of the rich to clear the caterpillars, and guard duty outside the village, and the struggle against locusts, and countless other "tasks" besides these, which make the villager feel like a beast of burden forever. Then there is the burden of unremitting toil in the soil and the fields, to supply maize for his food, if only he could do so for the whole year. Then there is the burden of tradition—especially on the woman—who is never more than a commodity in the eyes of the man. If she stays on good terms with her family and it is prosperous, then she receives some respect because there is money coming to her sometime, but if her family has been ruined—and many families have been ruined, as we have seen—then she suffers such humiliation and abuse as to turn her life into the blackest darkness.

Between that gloomy and oppressive sorrow and these "burdens of fate," the wrinkles on the face of fate opened up to show one smile. It was those children who romped and played for a large part of the year free of toil and labor until some time after their tenth year.

That was a quarter of a century ago. When the boy returned to his beloved village for a visit and inquired among other things about the romping of the children, he was told that that is all finished. That last smile on the gloomy face of fortune has gone out. It is now too hard to earn a livelihood, so the children and young boys are no longer allowed to laugh and romp and play, but are sent to work in the fields from the age of seven or eight, and their innocent gatherings and beautiful games have vanished from the village. This age has overburdened them and scourges their backs to drive them to labor from a young age. The whole "burden of fate" is on one shoulder, while on the other shoulder is the law of compulsory education, which takes the children from their work and thus takes the snacks out of their mouths while giving them neither knowledge nor food!

12   The Journey

The time came for him to leave the village, for he could no longer remain there. There was a task that awaited him, and he was like a soldier prepared for the struggle, drafted for this task, which his mother
had both prepared him for and hidden from him from the first day he
was taken to school. Then she had revealed it to him the day he came
in and saw her crying! He had to restore to the family the prestige and
money it had lost!

These were the words he heard from his mother as she prepared
him for the journey, the trip to his uncle in Cairo, where he would
study. He had already entered adolescence and had left the village
school two years earlier. Had it not been for the revolution, the
breakdown of communications, and disturbed conditions, he would
have traveled at that time. But now things had quieted down and he
had become strong, and the task for which he had been drafted urged
him on, so let him travel with the blessing of God.

The news got around to some of the women of the village who
were their friends, and they came. It was as if they had agreed beforehand what they would say, for their tongues all uttered nearly the
same words:

"Blessings on you, my sister, blessings. This little one is the one who will recover all that has been lost, and with God's permission will become . . . a 'somebody.' "

This fellow was now a man and was seen as a model around the village. His father had spent liberally on him so that he got his diploma at the same time as his father's wealth was almost ending. Then, "May God grant him success," as they say in the village. "May his fame soar and may good fortune attend him, and may he recover the lost wealth and multiply it many times over." He became in his village and in the surrounding ones an example of joy following adversity, of the restoration of good families after their ruin.

Everything about the boy's trip suggested that he had a great task, even as if "he were going to conquer Acre!"[1] But this was one thing, and the parental worry over his departure was another. Even though his mother had been the one who kept urging him to make the trip and preparing herself for it and surrounding it with her dreams—she now realized that a real departure is quite different from a merely anticipated one. As for his father, he remained calm and amiable as long as he remained silent, but when he spoke, the words caught in his throat. So he stopped and did not finish what he wanted to say, for fear of embarrassing himself.

For breakfast his mother had made him a milk dish that he loved, which was called *rashta* in the village. It was made of strips of wheat dough that she flattened out into pancakes, then folded, then cut up in a special way with a knife into thin strips, and which she thoroughly cooked in milk and sugar. In the morning clarified or fresh butter was put on them. She had prepared this for him—and they all made a breakfast of it.

The plan was that he would travel to Cairo with an *effendi* who was studying in the final year of law and was related to their family by marriage. The *effendi* would deliver him to his uncle so that his parents could feel more confident about his trip. The *effendi* had also agreed to travel together with a student from the Azhar, in order to pass the time on the long train ride.

When the boy was nearly finished preparing his baggage, these two arrived and knocked at the door, telling him to get into the carriage, for the time had come to catch the train. The boy's feelings had been confused, his mind distraught, and his thoughts distracted. He did not know if he was happy with the trip to Cairo, of which he had dreamed for years, or sad at leaving the world that he had known for years. When the call came it rescued him from his distraction, and he rushed to take leave of his family, one by one. His mother embraced him and clasped him to her breast as if she were depositing within him all the warmth of her anxious heart. She did not let him loose until his father gently pulled him from her, stifling the words in his throat because the knocking and the calling continued.

Then he went out, and his father followed to bid him farewell. It was a hasty farewell, after which the boy unburdened himself and expressed freely the anxieties he had been suppressing. His mother and sisters looked at the platter that had been prepared for breakfast. They looked at it as if it were a last memento of the departing boy. They looked at it perplexedly for a long time.

It was a sacred memento or a guarded treasure. The father came back into the house. The mother said, her words quivering: "Has he gone?"

The father said: "With God's peace."

With that he burst out crying like a child. The brave mother forgot her own worries and consoled him! Then she went off alone where she too could cry without restraint.

 Notes

Dedication

1. First published in serial form in the popular magazine *al-Hilal*, 1926–27, the first part of Taha Hussein's autobiography was then published in book form in Arabic under the title *al-Ayyam* [The days] (Cairo: Maba'at Amin 'Abd al-Rahman, 1929). It was first translated into English by E. H. Paxton as *An Egyptian Childhood* (London: Routledge, 1932).

Translators' Introduction

1. D. Crecelius, "The Course of Secularization in Modern Egypt," in *Islam and Development*, ed. John L. Esposito (Syracuse, N.Y.: Syracuse Univ. Press, 1980), 61.

2. Dwight F. Reynolds, ed., *Interpreting the Self: Autobiography in the Arabic Literary Tradition* (Berkeley: Univ. of California Press, 2001).

3. Henri Habib Aryout, *The Egyptian Peasant* (1933; reprint, New York: Beacon Press, 1963), 111.

4. Tetz Rooke, *In My Childhood: A Study of Arabic Autobiography* (Stockholm: Almquist and Wiksell, 1997), 173.

1. The *Magzub*

1. *Hayy* is Arabic for "alive," referring to God, and is a common verbal ejaculation in Sufi *dhikrs*, the devotional exercise of "remembering" the divine reality.

2. *Wali* (pl. *awliya*). In popular Islam the "Awliya Allah" ("Friends of God") are re-

garded as persons of exceptional spiritual merit who intercede on behalf of the living and are able to perform miracles *(karamat)*. The classical reference is found in Qur'an 10:63: "Surely God's friends *(awliya)*—no fear shall be on them, neither shall they sorrow." *Awliya* are both acclaimed during their lifetimes and venerated after their deaths. Sometimes translated as "saints."

3. In traditional Middle Eastern Muslim cosmology, Mount Qaf is the cosmic mountain that encircles the world. Qutb al-Ghawth is one name for the *wali* that stands at the top of the invisible cosmic spiritual hierarchy that Sufis believe in.

4. *Magzub* (Egyptian pronunciation; in literary Arabic *majdhub*). In popular Islam, an individual deemed to be in a state of "divine attraction" *(gazb or jadhb)*, which absolves him or her from adherence to social norms. As Qutb here relates, the behavior of a *magzub* is often unconventional and even bizarre. See Valerie Hoffman's discussion of *gazb* in her *Sufism, Mystics, and Saints in Modern Egypt* (Columbia: Univ. of South Carolina Press, 1995), 208–13.

5. Ka'ba. The stone cubicle at the great mosque in Mecca, which according to the Qur'an was built by the Prophet Abraham as a shrine to God. The hajj is the pilgrimage to Mecca that Muslims are obliged to make at least once in their lifetimes if they are physically and financially able to do so.

6. 'Ifrit (pl. *'afarit*). Often translated as "demons" or "sprites." A class of beings, associated with the jinn, which are believed to originate from under the earth, where they form a society that mirrors that of humans. *'Afarit* are thought to haunt certain locations, particularly ones that are uninhabited or isolated from regular human traffic. See chapter 6, *'Afarit*.

7. The Well of Zamzam is situated a few meters to the east of the Ka'ba. Muslim tradition relates that the well was opened by the angel Gabriel, to save Hagar and her son Isma'il from dying of thirst in the desert.

2. The Gym Master

1. Al-Azhar is the great mosque-university at Cairo, founded in 969 C.E. Among Sunni Muslims, it is the most famous center of Islamic learning in the world. Its course of instruction revolved around the traditional religious sciences. Beginning in the early 1900s, reformers such as Shaykh Muhammad 'Abduh attempted with some success to pull al-Azhar in a new, more modern direction, chiefly by rationalizing its bureaucracy.

2. *Kuttab* (pl. *katatib*). The traditional elementary school of Egypt and other coun-

tries of the Muslim world, whose normal method of instruction was to inculcate within children extensive passages of the classical Arabic of the Qur'an. As is clear from what Qutb says, the *kuttab* formed an intrinsic component of the village social structure and ingrained rural customs and traditions. Peasants felt it both a social and a religious obligation to send their children to the *kuttab*, if only for a short while.

3. *Baraka*. Spiritual power, sometimes translated "blessing."

4. The *quftan* is a long-sleeved outer garment, open in front. The *gallabiyya* is a long, loose-fitting garment, shirt-like at the top but covering the whole body, commonly worn by Egyptian males.

5. *Faqib* (pl. *fuqaba*). Strictly speaking, an expert in Islamic jurisprudence (*fiqb*), but in popular usage a Qur'an reciter and a *kuttab* teacher (see note 2 above).

6. These commands are derived from Turkish, which, until the late nineteenth century, had been the language of the Egyptian state elite. Elements of the Turkish language survived among members of Egypt's military establishment well into the twentieth century.

3. The Sacred School

1. The Nationalist Party, lit. al-Hizb al-Watani, established in 1907 by Mustafa Kamil (1874–1908), called for the immediate evacuation of the British from Egypt. Kamil emphasized Egypt's place within the wider Ottoman and Islamic worlds, but was at heart an Egyptian territorial nationalist. He was the publisher of the nationalist organ *al-Liwa* (The Standard), which galvanized the Egyptian nationalist movement, especially following the Dinshaway episode of 1906.

2. *Mibrab*. A niche in a mosque indicating the *qibla*, or direction of prayer.

3. *Effendi* (lit. *afandi*). Term used to denote members of the modernizing middle class of Egypt and other Arabic-speaking countries. Typically, *effendis* were employed as civil servants and teachers and wore the tarbush and European-style trousers and jackets. The cultural and socioeconomic position of the Egyptian *effendiyya* is well treated in Israel Gershoni and James Jankowski, *Defining the Egyptian Nation, 1930–1945* (Cambridge, UK: Cambridge Univ. Press, 1995), 11.

4. Qutb is here referring to Asyut, capital of Asyut Province (Mudiriyyat Asyut). In Qutb's day, Asyut city had approximately 42,000 inhabitants.

5. 100 piastres (Arabic sg. *Qirsh*) is equal to one Egyptian pound. One piastre is made up of 100 milliemes.

6. A well-known figure in Egyptian folktales who gets himself out of difficult sit-

uations by his wits. For example, see *Folktales of Egypt*, ed. and trans. Hasan M. El-Shamy (Chicago: Univ. of Chicago Press, 1980), 4–14, 83–86.

7. *Mashallah.* Literally, "What God wills." An extremely common expression in Egypt, used usually for something unusual or admirable, though possibly for something unfortunate, because all things fall within God's will. Here used sarcastically.

8. These grammatical endings are associated with formal literary Arabic. They do not usually appear in the colloquial Arabic used in everyday speech.

9. 'Abu al-Qasim Mahmud Ibn 'Umar al-Zamakhshari (d. 1143). A theologian and philologist of the Mu'tazilite school whose commentary on the Qur'an, *al-Kashshaf 'an Haqa'iq al-Tanzil*, is widely read in Egypt and the countries of the Muslim East.

4. Medical Mission

1. *'Umda* (pl. *'umad*). A village headman, or mayor, responsible for such local administrative duties as the collection of agricultural taxes and the maintenance of order within the community. For his efforts, the *'umda* was exempted from corvée labor and other impositions levied by higher authorities upon the peasantry. In Qutb's time, the post was usually the prerogative of a single family.

5. The Local Doctor

1. These are Islamic festivals and celebrations. The Day of 'Ashura refers to the tenth of Muharram, the first month of the Islamic year, and is marked by Sunni Muslims with a voluntary fast; the greater 'Eid is the "Feast of Sacrifice" on the tenth of the month of Dhu al-Hijja, whose most important feature is the sacrifice of an animal (usually a sheep) in commemoration of the ram sacrificed by the Prophet Abraham in place of his son; the lesser 'Eid is the "Feast of the Breaking of the Fast" and occurs as soon as the new moon is sighted at the end of Ramadan, the month of fasting; Sha'ban is the eighth month of the Islamic calendar. According to popular belief in the night preceding the fifteenth of that month every human's fortune for the coming year is registered in heaven. The mercy of God also descends on this night and sinners who repent are likely to obtain forgiveness. The night is marked by prayer vigils and by fasting.

2. Here Qutb is referring to the similarity between the Arabic words *mashmum*, "smelled," and *masmum*, meaning "poisoned."

3. Sayyid al-Badawi (d. 1276) is the most popular saint of Egypt's Muslim population; his tomb at Tanta in the Delta is the focus of the largest pilgrimage in Egypt. Ibrahim al-Desuqi (d. 1288) was the founder of the Burhaniyya Sufi Order, popular in the Egyptian Delta. 'Abd al -Qadir al -Jilani (d. 1077), considered by many Muslims to be the greatest saint of Islam, gave his name to the Qadiriyya Sufi Order. Al-Qutb al-Mutawalli is the Qutb believed by many to reside behind the door of Bab Zuwayla, one of the gates of medieval Cairo, according to Edward Lane in *Manners and Customs of the Modern Egyptians* (London: Everyman's Library, 1936), 237.

4. See chapter 1, note 3.

6. The 'Afarit

1. See chapter 1, note 6.

2. *Zar.* A spirit-possession cult, popular among women, in which participants enter into trance to seek release from physical or mental ailments that they believe are caused by malevolent spirits. The ceremony is marked by rhythmic dancing and sometimes by a sacrifice.

3. For an informative ethnographic exposition of the *qarina*, see Winifred S. Blackman, *The Fellahin of Upper Egypt* (1927; Cairo: American Univ. in Cairo Press, 2000), 54, 64–ff., 69–ff., and passim.

4. The seventh day after a birth is marked by a ceremony that includes, in addition to the festivities described by Qutb, the bestowal of a name upon the child.

5. Qutb is here referring to his younger brother Muhammad.

6. Sura 112 and Sura 2, verse 255.

7. Cultural Activity

1. *Abu Zayd, Zanati Khalifa,* and *Diyab Ibn Ghanim* are heroes of the romance of the Banu Hilal, based on the tenth-century migration of a Bedouin tribe from Arabia to Ifriqiyya (Tunisia) via Egypt. Professional storytellers related the tales in coffeehouses. The Story of Zir Salim is a folk elaboration of the *Ayyam al-'Arab* ("Battle Days" of the pre-Islamic Arabs) and is the introduction to the epic cycle of the Banu Hilal. In the tale, Kulayb is portrayed as a noble warrior.

2. *Qasidat al-Burda,* by Muhammad al-Busiri (d. 1294), is a devotional poem in praise of the Prophet, composed in thanksgiving for the author's recovery from illness. A translation of this poem is found in Arthur Jeffery, ed., *Reader on Islam* ('S-

Gravenhage: Mouton, 1962), 605–20. For Ibrahim al-Desuqi, Sayyid al-Badawi, 'Abd al-Qadir al-Jilani, see chapter 5 n. 5. The Barmakids were a celebrated family of state secretaries and viziers under the early Abbasid caliphate. The Abbasids were the second caliphal dynasty. They ruled until the Mongol sack of Baghdad in 1258.

3. Amira Dhat al-Himma ("The High-minded Princess") and Muhammad al-Battal ("Muhammad the Hero") are the heroes of the *Sirat al-Amira Dhat al-Himma*, a romance inspired by the Arab-Byzantine wars.

4. *Dala'il al-Khayrat*, a handbook of prayers and invocations by al-Jazuli (d. ca 1465), which invokes blessings over the Prophet. Portions of it are translated in Jeffery's *Reader on Islam*, 530–36. For mid-Sha'ban, see chapter 5 n. 1. Laylat al-Qadr is associated with Ramadan, most usually with the 27th of that month, and marks the first revelation of the Qur'an.

5. Hamza Fath Allah (d. 1918) was an educator at Dar al-'Ulum (see note 15 below). The work in question, *al-Mawahib al-Fathiyya fi 'Ulum al-Lugha al-'Arabiyya*, took a traditional approach to grammar.

6. Antar is the famous pre-Islamic poet whose legends formed the basis of the romance *Sirat 'Antar*, which was recited by storytellers.

7. Abu Ma'shar (787–866), a Persian scholar who was renowned as the leading astrologer in the Islamic world, a reputation maintained in the Latin West, where he was known as Albumasar. See the translation of his *The Abbreviation of the Introduction to Astrology together with the Medieval Latin Translation of Adelard of Bath* by C. Burnet, K. Yamamoto, and M. Yano (Leiden: E. J. Brill, 1994).

8. Al-Bukhari (d. 870). Collector of *hadith*, traditions relating the Prophet Muhammad's sayings and deeds. Al-Bukhari gathered some three thousand "sound" *hadith* in his collection *al-Jami' al-Sahih*, to which Qutb here refers. This is one of the two most authoritative collections for Sunnis, the other being that of Abu Muslim.

9. Lane describes a similar method in *Manners and Customs of the Modern Egyptians*, 274 ff., as does Ahmad Amin, *Qamus al-'Adat wa al-Taqlid wa al-Ta'bir al-Misriyya* (Cairo: Lajnat al-Ta'lif wa al-Tarjama wa al-Nashr, 1953), 381.

10. These "words" are the letters of the alphabet grouped so as to be pronounceable. As the author indicates, they represent numbers and their order is based on that of the Hebrew alphabet, which is different from the usual order of the Arabic alphabet. This system is sometimes called *abjad* and in modern times may be used to number the introductions to books, where Europeans would use lowercase Roman numerals.

11. Maghribi, an individual from North Africa, specifically what is today Tunisia, Algeria, and Morocco.

12. 'Abbas Hilmi II, a member of the Muhammad 'Ali dynasty and the last khedive of Egypt, bore the popular title "Our Effendi," and was exiled by the British in 1914. 'Abbas Hilmi II was known for his willingness to challenge the British authority in Egypt, especially Lord Cromer, Britain's agent and consul general in Egypt from 1883 to 1907. Shaykh 'Abd al-'Aziz Jawish and Muhammad Farid succeeded Mustafa Kamil in 1908 as leaders of the Nationalist Party. Anwar Pasha Turki was the Ottoman war minister. Tal'at Bey was a founding member of the Committee of Union and Progress, which involved the Ottomans in the Great War on the side of the Central Powers. Ra'uf Bey was the Ottoman naval officer who became a national hero in 1913 as commander of the cruiser *Hamidiyya* during the Balkan Wars.

13. Muhammed Bey Khudari was later a well-known professor at Cairo University.

14. Muhammad Ibrahim Hafiz (d. 1932) and Ahmad Shawqi (d. 1932). Two of the most highly regarded neoclassical poets, who sought to revive the style and spirit of classical Arabic poetry. Of special interest to them were figures such as Abu Tamman, Abu Nuwwas, Bashashar Ibn Burd, and al-Mutannabi, acknowledged masters of the *qasida*, the old Arabic ode. The neoclassical poets emphasized national and Islamic themes. In the 1920s and 1930s, Qutb would follow representatives of a growing Romantic trend in Egyptian letters in opposing Hafiz, Shawqi, and other neoclassical poets.

15. Dar al-'Ulum. Cairo's teachers' training college, founded in 1872 at the behest of the Khedive Isma'il. Dar al-'Ulum combined "scientific" western-derived subjects with instruction in traditional Islamic studies. As Donald Reid writes, its primary purpose was "to provide what al-Azhar and the professional schools could not: men who could teach the humanities in Arabic with at least some reference to western scholarship." *Cairo University and the Making of Modern Egypt* (Cambridge, UK: Cambridge Univ. Press, 1990), 34. Sayyid Qutb studied at Dar al-'Ulum between 1929 and 1933.

16. Sa'd Zaghlul (1857–1927). Politician, nationalist, and founder of the Wafd Party, which was a vital force in Egyptian politics throughout the period of the Old Regime. Zaghlul was the upwardly mobile son of an *'umda* from al-Gharbiyya province. He studied at al-Azhar and at Cairo's French Law School and thereafter enjoyed a prominent career as a lawyer, judge, and government administrator. Following World War I, Zaghlul led a number of Egyptian notables in lobbying British officials for Egypt's independence. The group called itself the "Egyptian delegation" (*al-wafd al-misri*). The Wafd's message of national self-determination aroused popular

discontent at Britain's refusal to end the protectorate. Following Britain's exile of Zaghlul and two other Wafd members to Malta in 1919, the Egyptian population erupted in spontaneous rebellion, first in the cities and then in the rural districts. Qutb's autobiography provides us with a rare glimpse of the uprising at the village level. The ongoing disturbances prompted Britain unilaterally to grant Egypt partial independence in 1922. In 1924, Zaghlul became Egypt's first elected prime minister.

8. The Law of the Thieves

1. *Futuwwa.* A term derived from *fata* (pl. *fityan*), "young man," meaning "chivalry" or "manliness." In the medieval period, *futuwwa* referred to brotherhoods practicing a kind of chivalry and often associated with Sufism. Some modern writers use the term to describe young men living lives of delinquency, and this appears to be the sense employed by Qutb here.

2. Literally "Shari'a Court." Beginning in the nineteenth century, Egypt's modernizing rulers replaced much of Shari'a law, based on the Qur'an and the example of the Prophet, with European-derived legal codes, especially in areas pertaining to criminal, commercial, and administrative matters. Only in what is called "personal status" matters, mainly matters relating to the family, does Shari'a law, with some modifications, still apply. Until 1955 this law was applied in separate courts known as Shari'a Courts.

10. The Harvest

1. 'Amr Ibn al-'As (d. 663). The Muslim Arab warrior who "opened" Egypt to Islam in 640–42 and founded a garrison city at Fustat, near the future Cairo.

2. "The Feast of Sacrifice"; see chapter 5 n. 1.

12. The Journey

1. Acre was a fortress, regarded as the key to Palestine, held by the Crusaders from 1110 to 1187 and 1191 to 1291.

 # Glossary

'arif: A school monitor who assists the teacher of a kuttab.

Al-Azhar: The great mosque-university at Cairo. Among Sunni Muslims, it is the most famous center of Islamic learning in the world.

balila: Dish made of stewed wheat and salt.

baraka: Spiritual power, sometimes translated as "blessing."

battau: Bread made of pure maize or maize mixed with wheat.

dhikrs: Devotional exercises for "remembering" the divine reality, invocations of God.

effendi (in literary Arabic, afandi, afandiyya): Term used to denote members of the modernizing middle class of Egypt and other Arabic-speaking countries. Typically, effendis were employed as civil servants and teachers and wore the tarbush and European-style trousers and jackets.

faqih (pl. fuqaha): Strictly speaking, an expert in Islamic jurisprudence (fiqh), but in popular usage one who recites the Qur'an and teaches in a kuttab.

feddan: A unit of agricultural measurement, a little less than an acre, equivalent to 4,200.833 square meters.

fellahin (sing. fellah): Peasants.

futuwwa: The noble, chivalrous qualities of a man; name given to youth organizations.

gallabiyya: A long, loose-fitting garment, shirt-like at the top but covering the whole body, commonly worn by Egyptian males.

gazb or jadhb: state of "divine attraction."

hajj: the pilgrimage to Mecca that Muslims are obliged to make at least once in their lifetimes if they are physically and financially able to do so.

Hājj: Title for one who has made the pilgrimage at Mecca.

halla: A copper cooking pot.

hayy: Literally "alive"; used as a common verbal ejaculation referring to God in Sufi **dhikrs,** devotional exercise of "remembering" the divine reality.

Iblis: In Islamic terms, the chief demon, counterpart of the Christian and Judaic Satan.

idha: If, when.

'ifrit (pl. **'afarit**): Often translated as "demon" or "sprite"; one of a kind of being associated with the jinn, thought to haunt uninhabited or isolated locations. **'Afarit** are believed to originate from under the earth, where they live in a society similar to that of ancient Arab tribal groups. See chapter 6, "The *'Afarit.*"

iftar: The first meal after sunset during the fasting month of Ramadan.

jadhb: See **magzub.**

jahili: Barbarous and ignorant.

jubba: A long garment with long, wide sleeves, open at front.

Ka'ba: Literally "cube"; ancient holy building in the center of the great mosque at Mecca toward which Muslims turn in prayer.

kalla: Work gang.

karamat: Miracles.

khatma: Literally, "completion"; recital of the entire Qur'an, especially on festive occasions.

kishk: A dough formed of bulgur and sour milk, used in the preparation of other dishes.

kuttab (pl. **katatib**): The traditional elementary school of Egypt and other countries of the Muslim world, whose normal method of instruction is to inculcate within children extensive passages of the classical Arabic of the Qur'an.

lawh: A shovel.

lupine: A grain legume high in protein.

maghribi: An individual from North Africa, specifically what is today Tunisia, Algeria, and Morocco.

magzub (Egyptian pronunciation; in literary Arabic **majdhub**): In popular Islam, an individual deemed to be in a state of "divine attraction" (**gazb** or **jadhb**), which absolves him or her from adherence to social norms. As Qutb relates, the behavior of a **magzub** is often unconventional and even bizarre.

makhash: Storage space for crops.

ma'mur: District commissioner.

mandal: A small pitcher used in a magical procedure to discover a thief; also, the name of the procedure.

maqallaya: Small clay pans.

mawlid: Birth celebration, especially that of a **wali**. Mawlid al-Nabi is the birthday festival of the Prophet Muhammad.

ma'zun: Notary public.

mazyara: A wooden closet enclosing water jugs.

mihrab: A niche in a mosque indicating the **qibla** or direction of prayer.

mishmishiyya: Dried apricot cooked in water, sugar, and clarified butter.

mu'awin: Adjutant.

mukhammar: A leavened pastry made with wheat flour, clarified butter, and milk.

mulahiz: Superintendent.

mulukhiyya: A leafy summer vegetable popular in Egypt.

muzayyara: An 'ifrit that takes the form of a woman.

piastre (Arabic **qirsh**): A unit of the Egyptian currency. One hundred piastres equals one Egyptian pound. One piastre, in turn, is made up of ten milliemes.

qarina: Jinni "companion" to a woman.

quftan: A long-sleeved outer garment, open in front.

raghif: Pure wheat bread.

Ramadan: The ninth lunar month of the Muslim calendar, when Muslims are obliged to fast during the daylight hours.

rashta: A dish made of wheat dough cooked in milk and topped with butter.

rayyis: The one at the head, or in charge of, a group of people; a "boss."

sarbatiyyah: Those who clean out drains and sewers.

shahid: Martyr.

shaykh: A title of respect applied to village and tribal elders, religious scholars, sufi masters, and pious gentlemen

suhur: The last meal before daybreak during Ramadan.

sura (pl. **suwar**): Term used to refer to a chapter of the Qur'an.

tal'a: Literally, "coming forth" or "going up." According to Blackman (*The Fellahin of Upper Egypt,* 117), a visit to the graves of relatives or friends on a particular day of the week, Thursday or Friday, when the souls of the dead are believed to return to the grave. Sayyid Qutb's description is somewhat different.

taqiya: Cotton skullcap.

tarbush: Fez.

tazyira: Black dress, covered by a shawl that is dyed and starched.

'umda (pl. **'umad**): Village headman, or mayor, responsible for local administration.

umma: worldwide community of Muslims

wali (pl. **awliya**): In popular Islam, the **Awliya Allah** ("Friends of God") are regarded as persons of exceptional spiritual merit who are able to perform **karamat,** or miracles. **Awliya** are both acclaimed during their lifetimes and venerated after their deaths. Although the word is sometimes translated as "saints," **awliya** can have a dangerous side, not usually associated with Christian saints; see chapters 1 and 5.

watani: Homeland.

zar: Exorcisms characterized by trance-like music and dancing to ward off the negative effects of demonic possession.

zi'nina: A spinning top.